Return to the Beginning

Snapshots of the Church

Volume I

Joseph Giuffrida Jr.

This book or parts thereof may not be reproduced in any form, stored in a retrieval system, or transmitted in any form by any mean – electronic, mechanical, photocopy, recording, or otherwise – without prior written permission of the author, except as provided by United States of America copyright law.

♦♦♦♦♦♦♦♦♦♦♦♦♦♦♦♦♦♦♦♦♦♦♦♦♦♦♦♦♦♦♦

RETURN TO THE BEGINNING: SNAPSHOTS OF THE CHURCH

VOLUME I

♦♦♦♦♦♦♦♦♦♦♦♦♦♦♦♦♦♦♦♦♦♦♦♦♦♦♦♦♦♦♦

Cover Photography by Ashley Noble (www.adorellaarts.com)

Cover Graphic Design by Jeanine Giuffrida

Unless otherwise noted, all Scripture quotations are from the King James Bible.

Available @ Amazon U.S., Amazon Europe, Kindle, and hardcopy.

© 2015 by Joseph Giuffrida Jr.

All rights reserved

ISBN-13:978-0692356098
ISBN-10:0692356096

Contact Joseph Giuffrida Jr. at: newcovrealities@gmail.com

Acknowledgments

I would like to acknowledge my father for lending his editing expertise to this book. As a master communicator, he is always able to fine tune a thought and enhance an idea. I would also like to acknowledge my friend Jeff Warren for giving of his valuable time to further edit this book. I would like to acknowledge my sister Jessica for offering her assistance in the editing process. I would like to acknowledge Ashley Noble for her professional work in photographing the front and back cover. I would like to acknowledge Alexx Hemphill for so elegantly modeling the Bride of Christ on the front and back cover. Finally, I would like to acknowledge my sister Jeanine for her stellar graphic design work on the front and back of this book.

Dedication

For teaching me about Christ's Church

This book is dedicated to W. Nee

The mentor who I never knew

Table of Contents

Chapter One: Snapshots..1

Chapter Two: The Constitution of the Church.....................11

Chapter Three: The Only Foundation..............................23

Chapter Four: Being the Church....................................41

Chapter Five: Universal Church vs Local Church................51

Chapter Six: Sectarianism part I....................................63

Chapter Seven: Sectarianism part II................................79

Chapter Eight: The Church Meeting part I........................99

Chapter Nine: The Church Meeting part II......................117

Chapter One

Snapshots

Snap! The camera clicks and then reels, ready for the next shot. Meanwhile, a moment has just been captured, a person has been crystalized on film, a landscape has been preserved, and an object has been held. Each snapshot of a camera produces an image that serves to remind us of something or someone. Although time propels us into the future, the moment we captured cannot be lost, no matter how many events transpire afterwards. This metaphor describes God's original thought for the Church, captured by the pen of inspired writers. The Church was God's thought. Along with everything else that He created, the Church was in the mind of God before it ever manifested into time and space. His intention for the Church has not changed, not in two thousand years of man trying to change it. It is true that mankind has historically sought to change God's original thought when it comes to creation, the identity of man, the role of government, the institution of marriage, and a thousand other things. Still, God's truth is left for every generation to rediscover, no matter how muddied it became at the hands of unenlightened people. To ensure that God's original thought behind what He created stayed a reality for mankind, He has throughout each generation chosen guardians of that original idea – people who gained a revelation of the original intent of God. Once these guardians obtained that revelation, they would communicate it to the world around them. One of the first guardians was the apostle Paul, who was handpicked by the Lord to express more clearly than anyone else of his day the message, identity, and function of Christ's Church. Once this communication went forth – whether by preaching, by letter, or by demonstration of power – revelation came forth like the burst of light from a camera, capturing God's thought. God inspired counsels in later centuries to collect these snapshots and put them into one Book. This inspired Book is called the Bible, and it is in the New Testament that God's original thought for the Church is found.

Throughout the New Testament account, God's thought for the Church broke though the human experience like a beam of light into a dark room. Divine illumination filled the mind of man and surfaced through the pen of the writer, the voice of the teacher, and the travels of the apostle. We don't have every conversation that the early Church had, nor do we know all the issues that they encountered, all of the celebrations they organized, all of the persecutions they faced, or the names of every person who believe the Gospel. However, what we do have is what the Lord wanted us to know, the people He wanted us to understand, and the events that He saw fit to reveal to us. Furthermore, we have the specific details which the Lord inspired the writers of the New Testament to tell us concerning the way in which His Church should be established. And we have the majority of these snapshots recorded by the apostle Paul, along with those individuals who learned from him and who documented his apostolic journey. Even though Paul's ministry came into being a few decades after the day of Pentecost, he was still needed to present God's original thought on the Church, to the Church. The first believers heard the Gospel, they received instruction from Jesus' apostles, and they began to see their lives as connected to one another. However, as with any truth that we discover, they still were in need of more mature revelation that would reveal even more nuances emphasizing that truth. For example, the early Church believed that Jesus Christ brought salvation to mankind; the apostle Peter demonstrated that in his Pentecostal speech. However, they did not have the fuller revelation that Jesus Christ *included* all of mankind into His salvific work on the Cross. They needed Paul's expansive revelation on Christ's finished work to grow in their understanding of this truth.

Throughout the New Testament account, we find numerous snapshots of God's thought concerning the Gospel as well as the way the Church should live out that Gospel. What these snapshots serve to do for us today is present an opportunity for us to repent! Repentance is the gift which enables us to discover and rediscover the original thought of God. By repenting, our minds are changed, and when this happens, everything that we have believed – whether by religious tradition or by our own personal misunderstandings – becomes aligned with the truth that has always existed in God's mind. The most evident conflict that occurs in the process of our repenting is the fight between God's thought and the thought produced by our traditions.

Letting Go of Our Traditions

The apostle Paul speaks of "traditions" in two different ways. And the distinction he makes is crucial to make here in the beginning. As believers, there are two kinds of traditions that are passed down to us.[1] The first is mentioned in Galatians 1:14 when Paul says that he "profited in the Jews' religion above many my equals in mine own nation, being more exceedingly zealous of the *traditions* of my fathers." The word "traditions" here speaks of those precepts and teachings which were handed down orally from Moses to the Israelites, and then to subsequent generations, which were illustrating and expanding the written law. These teachings included the way in which the Israelites were to perceive the physical temple, the duties that were to be performed therein, and various ceremonial laws which were imposed on the people. Jesus spoke much about the traditions of the Jews in His earthly ministry. In Matthew 15, the Pharisees asked Jesus why His disciples "transgress the tradition of the elders" by not washing their hands before eating bread. Jesus immediately pointed out their hypocrisy. He first pointed them to the commandment that fathers and mothers must be supported financially. He then denounced the tradition which the Jews placed over that command – "For God commanded, saying, *'Honor your father and your mother'*; and, *'He who curses father or mother, let him be put to death.'* "But you say, *'Whoever says to his father or mother, "Whatever profit you might have received from me is a gift to God"* – *'then he need not honor his father or mother.'* Thus you have made the commandment of God of no effect by your tradition" (4-6, New King James Version). In other words, these Jews were relaxing God's original command to them concerning the supporting of parents, and were instead making a loophole for Jews not to support them! And this is precisely what man's tradition does. It takes God's original thought on something and changes it.

Every one reading this right now was born in the last 100 years. We were born into a culture that already possessed religious norms which we could hear, touch, and see. We grew up understanding "church" to mean something particular – whether a building we attended, a denomination we were a part of, or a group of people that met in some other geographic location. Most of us grew up seeing the church as an event, something that could be scheduled into a calendar and placed on a specific day of the week. We were a part of church services that looked a certain way, lasted a certain amount of time, and were all too predictable as far as the order of events. We used names like "Baptist" and "Catholic" and "Pentecostal" and "Charismatic" to describe what kind of church we were a part of. We viewed the role of the pastor, the role of the music, the way we were to dress, and how each person was to function, according to some creed or code of conduct. We grew up hearing religious catchphrases that could only be heard coming from the lips of Christians. Our minds were molded to view the Church and its function according to man-made tradition. In the Biblical sense, man's traditions are addendums and revisions to the original idea of a thing. This kind of tradition is what many of our parents passed on to us, and their parents passed on to them. Man's tradition is based upon what our particular religious gathering taught us. Man's tradition emphasizes "the way church has always been in our lifetime" as opposed to the way it began and was defined in the very beginning. We have been *shaped* by this kind of tradition, from the time we are infants to the time we are elderly. Man's tradition has a way of making our present, cultural and religious norms seem like Gospel. This tradition etches in stone what is truth. This tradition says "This is the way to walk!" "This is the way to teach!" "This is the way to live!" It blinds us to the idea that there is another way to do what we've always done. In Colossians 2:8, Paul warns us to "Beware lest any man spoil you through philosophy and vain deceit, after the *tradition of men*, after the rudiments of the world, and not after Christ." Here, Paul voices his great concern about man-made tradition entering the Church. Furthermore, understand that the tradition of men is "not after Christ." In other words, any form of writing, teaching, or actual practice that is not based upon God's original thought – Jesus Christ – is a worthless thing. No man has the ability to write or to rewrite God's original idea for anything! This is why it is so important to rediscover the snapshots which God laid out for us in His divine Photo Book.

The second tradition which Paul speaks of is found in 2 Thessalonians 2:15 where he says, "Therefore, brethren, stand fast, and hold the *traditions* which ye have been taught, whether by word, or our epistle." From this verse, it is clear that there is a tradition which we *need* to hold onto. In context, Paul is speaking about the specific words which he communicated to the churches. He would continually emphasize that his Gospel was the *only* Gospel that should be received. In other words, how he interpreted the Person of Christ and the work of Christ would be the measuring stick by which we would know the truth. He taught the churches their identity based upon that Gospel, as well as how to express their individual callings based upon that Gospel. The need to see Paul's revelation as the doorway to understanding the rest of the New Covenant writings and ideas is essential for us today. No other apostle in the New Testament was given the scope of revelation that Paul received about Christ and the Church. We have more snapshots of God's mind concerning the Body of Christ in Paul's letters then in any other. Upon reading all of his epistles, we find a great command coming from the apostle in regards to the way we are to meet, the content of our meetings, and the specific function of every believer. We also find a heavy emphasis on the history of the Jews, the effect of sin, and the actual effect that the Cross had on all of humanity. In order to discover God's original thought for the Church, we must be willing to go back, passed all of our man-made tradition, and return to the beginning.

Can we ask some honest questions? Is it possible that our current religious traditions which we have received from the previous generation are not based upon God's original thought for His Church? And is it possible that the religious environment that was already created when we were born is not based upon God's original intent for His Church? Are we willing to relearn God's idea of who Christ is, what He accomplished, what the Church is, what the Church is not, and how the Church is to actually function in the earth? Have we come to the point of realizing how strong a role tradition has played in our everyday experience? Do we ever ask the question "Why am I doing what I am doing right now?" Is it possible that all of our desires for future revival, reformation, and spiritual awakening can be found in an event that has already taken place 2000 years ago? Do we ever feel uneasy when we survey the spiritual climate of the

Church today? And if we go as far as to say that the Church is not operating the way it ought to be, are we willing to revisit the Photo Album that God has given us and relearn from the beginning? Much of the reformation that is needed today has as much to do with adding elements to our understanding, as it does removing old, traditions that become harmful ideas which keep us in a state of confusion, uncertainty, and immaturity.

This book is designed to discover God's original thought concerning His Church. It is intended to understand the mind of God captured by men and women 2000 years ago, which speaks to the foundation, identity, and function of the Church. This book is not a formula; rather, it seeks to recapture snapshots of our Biblical beginnings. Upon recapturing these images, we will be returning to the original thought and intent of God for the Church. We will gain a clearer revelation as to what Christ's life, death, and resurrection actually affected – a completely new species of people who live according to a heavenly kingdom, rather than a worldly institution. This book is not detailing separate truths, but rather truths that are to be taken *together*. Each chapter is a puzzle piece that when put together, reveals the identity of the Church, the way the Church is to function, and the mindset that those in the Church are to have. By studying our foundation as believers, as well as the root cause of our denominationalism, the purpose of ministry gifts, the fruit of ministry to every member, and so much more, we will hopefully manifest the clearest image of God's original thought. And if it were possible to take a picture, we will see no difference between us and of those we find in the original Photo Book.

Chapter Two

The Constitution of the Church

Heaven is a country. We don't often think of it that way, but recognizing this truth will empower us to live as citizens of that country. Heaven operates as a theocracy, having a king as its ruler. It has a constitution, territorial dimensions, citizens, and a government. As king of this territory, God desired to create a reflection of heaven upon the earth. He created earth to mirror the glory that could be found in heaven. He created an environment in which to place man, and gave him the ability to take dominion over everything that was created. Man would eventually form countries based upon his ability to conquer and control certain territory. Today, there are approximately 196 countries in the world, and in order for each to be considered a legitimate country, they had to meet requirements such as being a self-governing political entity, occupying territory that has internationally known borders, having a population of people who live there, an economy, and a government. One of the most important attributes of a country is that it possesses a constitution – a set of fundamental principles by which the collective group of people may be governed. These principles will become that people's *law*. Every country on earth needs some form of law in order to establish the kind of harmony within its territory that protects the citizens from evil and provides a framework for individuals to thrive in business and in personal life.

Now, in the middle of man's pursuits to form countries on the earth, God decided to form a people group who would become distinguished among all others through which He could demonstrate His nature to the entire world. He chose Abraham to be this people's natural father. The divine intent was that Abraham's descendants would see God as the provider of a heavenly government to be administrated on the earth, which would set them apart as a *heavenly people*. The Israelites were chosen to be a physical representation of God's goodwill toward all of humanity, carriers of the divine promises of God, and whose lineage would produce the Messiah.

Ultimately, the nation of Israel would become the physical representation of the spiritual organism we call "The Church." God brought the Israelites out of the bondage of Egypt just like He would bring the Church out of the bondage of sin. God gave the Israelites their identity through Moses' words,

"And ye shall be unto me a kingdom of priests, and a holy nation." Likewise, He revealed the identity of the Church through God's word to the apostle John, "Jesus Christ...hath made us kings and priests." God promised the Israelites a physical homeland called "The Promise Land" just as He would promise the Church a spiritual homeland called "Heaven." God gave to the Israelites His laws written on stone tablets; in the same way, He wrote His laws on the hearts of those in Christ's Body. God revealed Jerusalem as the very center of His purposes on the earth; He reveals the very center of the Church's hope as the New Jerusalem which comes out of Heaven. God wanted the Israelites to trust in His leadership, His provision, and His protection as their King, even as He desired that the Church see Christ as their leader, their provider, and their protector as King. Finally, the Lord called Israel a "holy nation" in the same way that He would call the Church a "holy nation."

The word *nation* came to English from the Old French word *nacion*, which in turn originates from the Latin word *natio* literally meaning "that which has been born."[1] Although the word "country" is often used interchangeably with "nation," there is a difference. A nation is a community of people who share a common language, culture, ethnicity, or history. Unlike a country, a nation does not necessarily need a government or territory to make it exist. This distinction between country and nation can be seen when studying Israelite history. They were clearly a nation before receiving their promised territory, before having a man to govern over them, and before being recognized by other countries as an official country. The Lord purposed it this way so that the Israelites would see God as their king, from whom their identity was formed.

The Old Covenant

The Lord Himself "birthed" the nation of Israel at the foot of Mount Sanai, after they were brought out from under the tyrannical rule of Egypt, and it was there that they were introduced to a covenant with God. A *covenant* is a binding agreement – a formal sealed contract between two living parties. The conditions of a covenant become *legally binding* because they are *enforced by law*. God's covenant with the Israelites would become their *spiritual constitution*, enforced by the Law of God. In essence, the 10 Commandments became the physical document which required their obedience. These Commandments are moral laws that have existed for eternity. Along with these Commandments, they received 613 ceremonial and judicial laws that were embedded into this newly found constitution. Although Moses was the man chosen to reveal this Law to Israel, the "framer" was God. We know this because Exodus 31:18 declares, "And he gave unto Moses, when he had made an end of communing with him upon mount Sinai, two tablets of testimony, tables of stone, *written with the finger of God.*" This divinely initiated covenant would become Israel's constitution, designed to govern them for an appointed time.

The first place we see God referring to the Israelite people as a "nation" is in Exodus 19:6. This was part of God's prophetic word to Moses about the Israelites – that they would become "a holy nation" upon receiving this covenant. Before the giving of the Law, the Israelite people were simply known as the "children of Israel." This is significant as we see the giving of the Law to Israel as their defining moment and inauguration into nationhood. This is also significant in that they did not have a territory or earthly government which is needed to establish a country. God was demonstrating that this chosen people would exist as an extension of His heavenly government, and as representatives of the way in which God rules the heaven and earth. In order for them to uphold their end of the divine agreement, they would be required to obey the Law of God. To demonstrate their commitment to this pact, the Israelite people verbalized their willingness to do all that God required of them (see Exodus 19:8).

Hebrews 9:18 declares "Therefore not even the first covenant was dedicated without blood." Right after the Law was given to the Israelites, Moses took the blood of calves and goats and sprinkled them onto the book of Law as well on the people.

The word "dedicated" means "to initiate or to consecrate." In modern language, we might say that the covenant was "ratified" by the blood sacrifice of animals. The word "ratify" means "to sign or give formal consent to a treaty, contract, or agreement, making it officially valid." Because this agreement was ratified by the blood of animals, man could not be redeemed from his cursed state. It was a temporary atonement that covered their sin, yet did not remove it. Man needed divine blood in order to be redeemed from his cursed state.

Hebrews 9:16 says that "For where a testament is, there must also of necessity be the death of the testator." Since no human died in order to ratify the Old Covenant, we know that it was *not a testament*. And herein is the fundamental difference between a *testament* and a *covenant* – a testament is only enforced when the testator has died, and a covenant is an agreement between two living parties. The testament is a type of *will* which allows those stated in it to receive whatever the testator has designated to them after his or her death. Under the constitution that was ratified for the Israelites, there was a verbal agreement on God's part and on man's part. Therefore it remained only a covenant. Under this

> *The Israelites would not receive blessings from the Lord as an inheritance, but as a direct response to their obedience to God's Law*

verbal contract, *the Israelites would not receive their blessings from the Lord as an inheritance, but as a direct response to their obedience to God's Law*. This is why we find the phrase "If you will…" over and over again throughout the dispensation of Law. The fundamental problem which Israel faced was that they could not keep the Law perfectly, and therefore they were continually coming in and out of God's protection and provision.

It is true that God gave the Law as a means to bring fallen humanity to an end of itself. Romans 8:3 declares that the Old Covenant contained "fault" because it was "weak through the flesh." Since man could never fully obey all of God's requirements, the covenant itself would reveal man's inherent weakness in trying to perfectly fulfill God's Law. Under the external system of moral requirements, Israel was doomed to fail in their attempts to be like God. And this is exactly where the source of man's first sin could be found – attempting to become like God through self-effort. The Old Covenant would both succeed in amplifying man's failed attempts to become like his Creator, and God's wisdom in bringing this fallen mindset to an end. This is why the entire world needed nothing short of a resurrection from the dead, a new birth – a new constitution.

The New Covenant

The Birth of Jesus Christ marked the prophetic fulfillment of many prophecies given by men like Isaiah, Micah, and Jeremiah. Jesus was the God-Man who was sent by the Father to redeem the entire world and to usher humanity into the New Covenant. The fundamental difference in this new agreement was that God would *not* make a covenant based upon man's ability to uphold his end – God would make this covenant knowing that He would fulfill man's end! The New Covenant would be the result of Jesus fulfilling the Law of God for mankind as mankind. This is precisely why God became a man, so that all of mankind might become reconciled back to God. Man would not find his inclusion into this covenant based upon his verbal consent, nor by his physical choosing – the only way into this covenant would be *through faith* in what Jesus Christ accomplished to make the eternal reality of our union with God a reality in our minds.

In addition to a covenant, God would be giving mankind a *testament*. Since the giving of this testament would necessitate the death of the testator, God would have to die! Jesus – who was fully God – was born into the world in order to be the will of God, to do the will of God, and to give the will of God to mankind at His death. During the Last Supper, Jesus made a profound statement about the bread and the wine of which He and His disciples partook. "And He took bread, and gave thanks, and break it, and gave unto them saying, this is my body which is given for you: this do in remembrance of me. Likewise also the cup after supper, saying, *"This cup is the new testament in my blood*, which is shed for you" (Luke 22:19-20). Notice how Jesus said that the New Testament was *in His blood*. The blood of Jesus contains the very will of God for humanity! And since that will has already been enforced by His death, not only have we received our inheritance, but that inheritance has been supernaturally fused into our spiritual DNA. By our union with Christ's divine life, we have become co-heirs with Him to everything that belongs to the Father.

> *The New Covenant would be the result of Jesus fulfilling the Law of God for mankind as mankind*

Now the "declaration of independence" that Jesus proclaimed over humanity was that they had been freed from sin. The irony of this "declaration" is that, whereas mankind has been liberated from the sinful nature, mankind has also been liberated from the false mindset of self-government, reuniting us as dependents upon God. Jesus was the "violent man" who took the kingdom by force as He went to the Cross to remove us from everything that kept us from freedom, and simultaneously reuniting us with our true identity as sons of God.

It is important to see that whereas the Old Covenant emphasized the *outward* part of man, including outward obedience, outward worship, outward sacrifice, the New Covenant emphasizes the *inward* part of man, highlighting the "obedience of faith" found in the heart, and the worship that proceeds out of the heart. God did not exchange His heart and mind with ours so that we could try to obey Him, try to choose what is right, try to produce the kind of life that pleases God – *we have been given His very life* and therefore it is His faith, His obedience, and His worship that manifests through us. Since the constitution of the New Covenant has been written on our hearts and our minds, the outworking of it happens subconsciously as it flows out from our divine DNA. Under the New Covenant, we were never meant to be governed by the external rules and regulations that the Israelites were under, nor were we meant to be governed by the external impetus to keep the moral law of God, especially as it was continually communicated by men such as Moses, Samuel, and Josiah. We have received the government of God *within us* as well as the Holy Spirit who is *the Governor* of God's government! We are now governed from within by the perfect Law giver Himself – The Holy Spirit who perfectly fulfilled *every* righteous requirement of the Law in the life of Jesus Christ.

In his second epistle, the apostle Peter declares: "But you are a chosen generation, a royal priesthood, *a holy nation*, a peculiar people..." Notice how Peter is calling the Church a "holy nation." It is of supreme significance that the Church is considered a *nation*, as we know that every nation must be birthed into existence. The Church is a *spiritual body of people* that was formed outside of time and space – by God Himself – even as Eve was created from out of Adam's side, completely by God, and completely apart from Adam's doing. We did not physically come together at the Cross, but spiritually, all of humanity was *in Christ* as He was reconciling the world to Himself (see 2 Corinthians 5:19). As we have seen before, the word *nation* means "to be born." The Church was literally *born into existence at the resurrection of Christ*. All of humanity was gloriously included in the vicarious life, death and resurrection of Christ, and therefore it was at the point where He was "born" from out of the grave that the Church became "born again." This is the mystical reality that we are a part of – that our new birth did not happen by our own will, nor did it occur in space and time. It was a reality that existed in Christ from before the foundation of the world, culminating in the resurrection of Jesus Christ, and manifesting in our physical existence in time-space.

The Church now shares the same culture, language, ethnicity and history. The work of the Cross engraved the writing of this new nation's constitution on the tables of our hearts and minds – the Law of God has been written within us.

We have been made citizens in the country of Heaven, called to speak the same language, woven into the DNA of Jesus Christ, all having been birthed at the resurrection of Christ. Paul says that we are all to be of the same mind – dwelling on heavenly things. We are a heavenly society, a royal class of kings and priests, called to declare the finished works of Jesus Christ. As ambassadors of our new country, we must come to fully accept all that God did to include mankind into the Godhead. We must fully accept the indescribable grace of God that is so eloquently laid out in the New Covenant writings of Paul, Peter, James, John and Jude. We must also see that the constitution of the Church sums up our complete existence, our total redemption, our very livelihood, and that only in the life, death, and resurrection of Christ can we truly comprehend our completed perfection and citizenship in Heaven.

Chapter Three

The Only Foundation

The foundation of all ministry, of all teaching, of all mission-centered work, and of all practical living, is found in the person of Jesus Christ. The apostle Peter tells us that we – the Church – are the living stones which make up the temple of God. Therefore, Christ is the foundation on which every stone is built. All that we do must be built upon the revelation of Jesus Christ, even as Peter's ministry would be built upon his revelation of the Christ (see Matthew 16). In today's Church culture, we have had so much exposure to "every wind of doctrine" – from TV personalities, radio broadcasts, Sunday morning guest speakers, and those whom we call "pastor." We have heard conflicting messages from a myriad of different people, to the extent that a false foundation has been laid in our minds. Many cannot say with certainty what they believe about the core doctrines including salvation, the Old and New Covenants, the nature of sin, and the finished work of the Cross. This is because they have not had the *right foundation* to interpret such glorious truths.

When speaking of foundations, the apostle Paul makes this important statement: "For we are laborers together with God, ye are God's husbandry, ye are God's building. According to the grace of God given unto me, as a wise master builder, I have laid the foundation, and another buildeth thereon. But let every man take heed how he buildeth thereupon. *For other foundation can no man lay than that is laid, which is Jesus Christ*" (1 Corinthians 3:9-11). It is significant that Paul – the "wise master builder" of the Church – would make the exclusive claim that there is *no other foundation* which can be laid than that of Jesus Christ. Paul does not say that the mere knowledge of Christ is our foundation, but that *the person* of Christ is the foundation we must receive. By saying that he was a "master builder," Paul was not asserting that he built physical temples; he was revealing the very definition of the minister's work – *to lay the revelation of Christ in the minds of people.*

Paul makes two statements that are of note when considering the correct foundation which we are to have as the Church. The first is in Galatians 1:1 where he says, "Paul, an apostle, (not of men, neither by man, but by Jesus Christ, and God the Father, who raised him from the dead)." Notice how his ministry of apostleship was not given to him "of men" or "by man." Human cleverness, intellectual ability, and self-effort can never be the foundation for a person's ministry. The power needed to demonstrate our callings must come from heaven, and be sourced in the person of Christ. The second is found in verses

11-12 where he says, "But I certify you, brethren, that the gospel which was preached of me is not after man. For I neither received it of man, neither was I taught it, but by the revelation of Jesus Christ." Here we find the message of this apostle having not originated in the mind of man, or from the order of mankind – it was revealed when the person of Christ was revealed. When we consider these two passages, it is clear that both *Paul's ministry* and *Paul's message* originated in the person of Jesus Christ.

> *The very definition of the minister's work is to lay the foundation of Christ in the minds of the people*

The Gospel that Paul preached was not a product of human ingenuity: it was not manufactured by human minds – Paul's Gospel was received as soon as he was introduced to Christ! By this we must see that the Gospel is not merely teaching *about* Jesus Christ, but that *the Gospel is the revelation of Jesus Christ.* The foundation which Paul was laying in those he was sent to revealed the personality of God which could be tangibly experienced. He was not coming to the people with a theological degree, but with the manifest substance of the One he was preaching.

A Christological Perspective

The Bible is not and was never intended to be read as though it were merely telling of random, historical accounts centering on mankind. Although the Bible is a written account detailing the lives of hundreds of men and women from different time periods and from different cultures, it has a singular focus. Whether dealing with Adam, the Israelite nation, the Levitical laws (which included animal sacrifices and temple worship performed by the ordained priesthood), the men and women of faith who adorn the pages of the Old Covenant, or the many prophets who came to announce the coming of the Messiah, the entire Bible is a divinely inspired account through which mankind may see the Christ. From cover to cover, we are gaining revelation that reveals the Anointed One – His character, His will, His purpose, His design, His people, His accomplishment, His sovereignty, and His power. We are not introduced to the myriad of people recorded – their traditions, cultures, and the specific ages which they lived in, so that we can base our understanding of God on humanity's character, will, purpose, and so on. We do learn a great deal about the nature of man throughout Scripture, however, we must see the highest purpose of these many accounts as only being types and shadows of the One who would reveal our true identity as His sons and daughters. Christ would literally embody the mystical union between God and man, and therefore show us the kind of union God has always intended to have with mankind.

Upon seeing Christ, we see the sum of all godly doctrine in Scripture. And only through having a Christological foundation can we properly interpret the mind of God concerning biblical doctrines. The word "Christology" literally means "the study of Christ." When studying Scripture, our aim should be to find what each passage reveals about the nature of Christ – particularly how Christ embodied the solution to the problem, the answer to the prayer, the victory to the battle, the Person to the physical symbol. The mistake that many have made is to look at various passages of Scripture, and attempt to interpret and teach the various texts through an anthropological view. The word "anthropology" means "the study of humankind." The emphasis of the anthropological view is always the individual, their struggle, their prayer, their attempt to win battles, their "part to play." When adopting this view in theological study, people will often place God and man in two separate categories, and attempt to derive God's role and man's role as two separate roles. What these people forget is all throughout Scripture, whenever it seems as though God is giving man a "part to play," man has always been dependent upon God's ability *through him* to accomplish what God says. Furthermore, the giving of the Law was clearly given to the Israelites for the purpose of them fulfilling each command. However, we know from studying the full counsel of Scripture that God gave this Law as a means to show Israel that *they could not fulfill the Law in their own strength.* And so, even in the passages of Scripture that seem like man has some role separate from God, we find it is not possible for a man to do the smallest thing – whether breathing, building, or battling – apart from the power which emanates from the Person of God.

We may also see the error of interpreting Scripture from anthropological mindset when considering the numerous types and shadows laid out in the Old Covenant which clearly point to the Christ. For example, there were various ceremonial steps which the Israelites were required to take in order to atone for their sins. Many still use this and other Levitical practices to draw a parallel with the New Covenant believer. Instead of teaching how Christ became our washing, our blood sacrifice, and our way into the Holy of Holies, they lay out steps and formulas regarding how we ought to live so that we may be able to approach God. Another example of this error is to see the many prayers prayed in the Psalms as prayers that are still acceptable for the New Covenant believer. For example, David prayed in Psalm 51:10 "Create in me a clean heart, O God; and renew a right spirit within me." This was prayed by a man who did not have a revelation of what we have today – namely that Christ *gave us a new heart and His very own Spirit!* This kind of prayer that is typical in the book of Psalms focuses on man's need for something only God can give; however, the greater revelation that mankind has been given since the Cross, is that

God *has already given us everything that we will ever need in Christ!* The former perspective is man-focused, the latter is Christ-focused. The former sees man's lack, the latter sees God's supply.

We will now mention just a few examples of interpreting Scripture from a Christological perspective. 1 Corinthians 1:30 declares that Jesus *became* our wisdom, righteousness, sanctification and redemption. Notice how wisdom is not a mere intellectual assent toward something, but is a personification of Christ! Righteousness is not merely a gift given to us by God – it is the very Person of God! Sanctification is not a process by which we become holy – it is the very Person of Christ, in whom is the very essence of holiness! Redemption is not something Jesus merely gifted us with after He died – He *became* our redemption! In John 6:35, Jesus said that He is the "bread of life" which reveals Him as our natural and supernatural sustenance. In John 7:38-39, Jesus declares His Spirit to be "rivers of living water" which reveals Him as our soul's satisfaction. In John 8:12, Jesus proclaims that he is the "light of the world" which reveals Him as our illumination into the God-realm. In 2 Timothy 2:13, Paul says that the nature of Christ is "faithful" which reveals Him as our trustworthy friend. We may consider all of the names of God as mystical doorways, all leading us into the glorious revelation of the very Person of God. Now, there is nothing wrong with studying mankind, his condition before and after "The Fall," and how he has interacted with God. However, mankind's experience, mankind's efforts, and mankind's finite perceptions can *never* be the foundation of the Gospel which we are to receive and preach.

Christ's Earthly Life vs. Christ's Eternal Life

At this point, it is important that we draw a distinction between Jesus' earthly life and His eternal life. As a man with physical flesh, He lived a physical life and died a physical death. As a man, he tasted death for all men (see Hebrews 2:9); however, as an eternal Spirit, He could not be held by death. Rather, He was resurrected by the eternal life within (see Acts 2:24). Jesus lives having a resurrected body and fully possessing the Spirit of God within Him (see 1 Corinthians 15:42). It serves to show us that Jesus' thirty three years on earth was for a specific purpose – a limited mission based in time and space to affect the eternal condition of mankind. Once Jesus died, His earthly ministry was finished. This is why, on the Cross, He cried out "It is finished!" The word "finished" in the Greek language is *teleo* which means "to perform, complete, fulfil; to do just as commanded, and generally involving the notion of time, to perform the last act which completes a process, to accomplish."[1] Jesus' earthly life and death marked the fulfillment of His mission. And therefore, we must see that His earthly ministry had the strokes of finality on it, one that could not be reproduced, added to, or taken away from.

There is a clear distinction between the physical life of Christ which existed for a specific purpose in a limited amount of time, and the eternal life of Christ which has always existed, before, during and after the physical Incarnation. If we do not rightly divide this fundamental difference, we will stray into all kinds of theological errors which can do great damage to our spiritual and natural lives, as well as in those to whom we minister. Jesus' earthly ministry wasn't just "the next big thing to happen" on God's timeline for humanity. Jesus' earthly ministry was and is the very essence of God's eternal plan for all of mankind. In Genesis 3, we find the first prophecy recorded in Scripture. We read of the divine plan to bring a Savior into the world whose salvific work would crush the workings of the devil. In Revelation 13:8, at the very end of the Bible, we find one angel declaring that Jesus was "the lamb slain from the foundation of the world." And again, in Revelation 14:6 we find another angel declaring the "everlasting Gospel." From beginning to end, we are reading about the

> *We must see that His earthly ministry had the strokes of finality on it, one that could not be reproduced, added to, or taken away from*

eternal nature of Christ's life and work. Therefore, one cannot simply make His earthly ministry the focus of the Gospel.

Now, it was the same eternal Spirit within Jesus that raised His body from the grave, who is now living within us. The great ambition which the apostle Paul had for the churches was to impart the revelation that *Christ was in them*! Surely, this had to be one of the most stunning revelations ever taught or heard – that God was not to be approached from behind a veil, or that He lived in a physical building, but that God actually resided within man!

The Apostle's Doctrine

In Acts 2:42 we find the early church continuing "steadfastly in the apostles' doctrine." Now, it is important to note that the apostles of Christ – those who walked with Him in His earthly ministry, were "unlearned and ignorant men" (see Acts 4:13). They did not attend the schools of the Law which their Jewish contemporaries had attended. They were unskilled in the Mosaic training which was typical for the priesthood of their day. The "doctrine" which they preached was not a product of intellectual learning, but of being eyewitnesses to the Son of God. They preached a message that was not aimed at getting people to follow the physical Lord – He had already ascended into heaven to which they were all eyewitnesses – but to reveal Christ as the long awaited Messiah. Their message did not reveal Christ as merely some great historical figure, neither were their words aimed at reiterating what He had spoken through His thirty-three years as a man. Their great commission was to tell the whole world of eternal life available through the eternal Spirit of Christ. Peter's message to Cornelius, Philip's preaching in Samaria, and Paul's preaching throughout Asia were all aimed at revealing the *eternal* life of Christ. Doctor Luke details this truth as he records that Philip *"preached Christ,"* and again that Paul *"straightaway...preached Christ."* He records Peter as saying *"And He shall send Jesus Christ, which before was preached unto you."* And again, Paul saying *"I have fully preached the gospel of Christ,"* and *"Now if Christ be preached,"* and *"Jesus Christ, who was preached among you..."* and *"whether in pretense or in truth, Christ is preached."* The language of Luke conveys the same thought that we find in the epistles of Paul, James, Peter, Jude, and John – Christ's eternal life is the subject of the apostolic doctrine. By saying that these men "preached Christ" he was revealing that these men were preaching the *entirety* of Christ's existence – not merely his teaching during His three and half years of ministry, but the eternal aspect of who He is and what He did to affect an eternal change upon all of humanity.

The "doctrine of Christ" which the apostle's preached was not the doctrine of what Jesus said, but the doctrine of *who He was and is*. Let me further explain. What is fascinating about studying the New Covenant writers (those men who laid out the revelation of Christ to the Church after Christ's ascension, including Paul, Peter, James, John and Jude) is discovering their omission of Jesus' earthly sayings! In fact, there are only two recorded places after Jesus' ascension that we find His disciples quoting from his earthly ministry. The first is found in Acts 11:17 where Peter is recounting the outpouring of the Spirit upon the Gentiles, and using Jesus' words to support the occurrence, saying "John indeed baptized with water, but you shall be baptized with the Holy Spirit." The second is found in Acts 20:32 where Paul is referring to the words of Jesus saying "It is more blessed to give than to receive." What's interesting here is that this particular quote was not recorded in any of the four Gospels. It is apparent that apostolic preaching was meant to highlight the eternal nature of Jesus' eternal life. Only Jesus could fulfill what He taught, as he was perfectly God and perfectly man. The Christological perspective we went over earlier reveals that Jesus has been made *everything* for us. The apostle John says "...as he is, so are we in the world." Jesus lived as a man, on behalf of mankind, to make all men just as He is. And this is the powerful truth which the apostles preached throughout the world – Christ offered Himself for all of mankind, to reveal Himself as mankind's true nature and identity. He therefore eliminated man's striving to emulate His life by *giving man His life*.

Today, most believers are aware that Jesus' ministry was reserved for Him, that only He could carry out the role of Savior. However, many have become intolerant of any idea suggesting that Jesus' earthly teachings were exclusively dealing with those under the Old Covenant. What they do not understand is that His words were designed to frustrate them, who by self-effort imagined that they could fulfill those words. It is said to be a radical notion that what Jesus taught – for example on the Mount of Olives – is not for the New Covenant believer to try to emulate and obey. Now, we are not advocating the removal of Jesus' earthly teachings from the mind of the believer, however it is of utmost importance that we see His teachings in the right context. After the spiritual rebirth, man would be able to reflect Jesus' righteousness, but it would come through faith and not by self-effort. Paul encapsulated Jesus' ministry this way: *"But when the fullness of the time was come, God sent forth his Son, made of a woman, made under the law, To redeem them that were under the law, that we might receive the adoption of sons."*

Notice here the purpose to which Jesus was born, and the purpose to which His earthly ministry would be released. He was born a man so that He could usher mankind out from under the grip of the Law which condemned them, and to bring them under the power of grace which would reveal them as sons of God. When Jesus taught, He taught predominately the Law of Moses. This is because He was speaking to Jews, and as such, those who knew the Law and those who tried to be justified by keeping the Law. Only through Jesus' perfection in keeping the Law could mankind experience freedom from the condemnation that ensued upon their breaking of that Law. Obviously, Jesus' ministry was not a ministry that anyone could actually perform. It would therefore be a monumental mistake to separate Jesus' ministry from His teachings. We could not fulfill His high priestly role as Savior, and neither could we fulfill His teachings. The reality is that Jesus' words could not be obeyed perfectly, and therefore even His teachings would ultimately condemn those who tried to follow them. We know this to be true as all of His closest disciples forsook Him in the end. This is why His teachings and His death on the Cross have to be seen as one inseparable ministry that could only be carried out by His perfect obedience. Jesus was manifest to take away the sin of the world; and the only way to accomplish this mission would be to render all self-effort useless in removing the eternal weight that sin placed upon each soul.

The preachers and teachers of the Church communicated the *finished work of Christ* – the *complete package* if you will – and therefore did not emphasize what Jesus said, but rather what Jesus did. If our foundation is simply the teachings of Jesus in His earthly ministry, we will soon find ourselves in a world of frustration. Jesus' earthly teachings were not designed to make men holy, but to frustrate mankind's ability to become like God through the human effort required by the Law. Hence, Jesus was focused on transitioning Jewish listeners into the New Covenant – a covenant which would not be based upon their obedience, but upon *His* obedience. Out of all the apostles, Paul especially understood the exclusive nature of Jesus' earthly ministry. Jesus spoke the words "The greatest commandment of the Law is to love the Lord your God…and to love your neighbor as yourself." Jesus' earthly ministry revealed that only He could perfectly love God and love His neighbor. There has been a divine infusion of God's love in us now that Christ has fulfilled that law. Paul understood that if the early Church grasped Jesus' divine work upon the earth – as mankind's substitute – they would begin to exhibit the life of God which loves perfectly.

The Right Foundation

The foundation of any building must be laid before any further structure can be built. Christ must be our foundation before we recognize our identity and the identity of everyone else who make up the spiritual structure called the Church. The revelation of who Christ is, the work that He has accomplished, and the eternal life which He gave us becomes the divine foundation which spreads out and touches each corner of our consciousness. We are then able to see our eternal perfection apart from our works, and our inclusion into the Godhead. We are able to identify ourselves as sons of God. We are able to recognize our freedom from sinfulness. Our minds are enlightened to see ourselves as having been crucified with Christ before we were even born. We are able to comprehend that our resurrection from the dead occurred before we took our first breath. We are able to glimpse into eternity and see ourselves in God before the foundation of the world. We can then become living letters which express the finished work of Christ in our daily experience. The foundation of Christ becomes the basis for which we minister our gifts to the Church, show forgiveness to the offender, love our children unconditionally, give of our money without hesitation, love ourselves without shame, build our businesses without greed, create an environment in which everybody may feel the love of God, and experience continual peace in the midst of the world's greatest troubles.

Chapter Four

Being the Church

Going to Church vs Being the Church

There is a popular phrase that has been circulating throughout the Church which has become the confession of many Christians in the U.S., "We don't go to church, we are the church." This statement has become a kind of politically correct way to describe the modern-day Christian's view of who he or she is in relation to the local church. And yet if we listen, we can hear the same people asking the question to others, "what *church* do you go to?" to which we will inevitably hear something like, "Oh, I attend (enter denominational, 501c3, overtly religiously titled organizational name, *here*). It is true that agreeing with the declaration "we don't go to church, we are the church" reveals our belief that Christ's Church is not a physical structure, but a spiritual Body. This statement also assumes that Christ did not create some natural, physical organization, but that He created an entirely new spiritual species. And since this mystical creation is made up of people – in whom Christ dwells – it is perfectly scriptural to say that we don't go to church, but rather have *become* the Church. However, agreeing with this declaration must consequently eliminate the question "what church do you go to?" as well as the answers "I attend such and such church" and "I am going to such and such a church." This is because they are actually affirming the false idea that Christ's Body is an earthly organization, in a particular location, or even some man-made entity which people can physically attend. When confronted about this contradiction, many of the same people who boldly proclaim "we don't go to church, we are the church" are the same ones who will dismiss this distinction as some minor technicality. Through their words and actions they will flat out deny their original consent to the truth that "we don't go to church, we are the church" by continuing to ask the question "what church do you go to?" and by making the statement "I attend such and such church."

And then there are those who ignorantly agree with the truth that "we don't go to church" and so, will instead replace the word "church" with "house" or "house of worship." They rightly see the Church as being more of a family than some rigid organization and will see this word-change as fitting the biblical outline more closely. You may hear them ask the more personal and unassuming question, "What *house of worship* do you go to?" Notice here that the question is not about a "church" but about a "house of worship." Many believe that to say "We are part of such-and-such church" is a denominational idea, but to say "we are part of such-and-such house of worship" is somehow acceptable. After all, the word "house" is closely associated with the idea of family – and we all know that the Church of Christ is a spiritual family. The fact that the phrase "house of worship" is used does not change the basic order of their church meetings; it simply makes the idea of meeting more tolerable as it does not sound as denominational as saying "we go to such-and-such church."

And still, there is another idea circulating in Christendom, which suggests that we are not to call ourselves "churches" or "houses" but rather "fellowships." We hear the line "What *fellowship* do you go to?" In this case, the word "fellowship" is personal, similar to "house" with more of a friendship-vibe to it. After all, we are all part of the fellowship of Christ and of His Gospel. The question remains, do these names – church, house, and fellowship – actually have any bearing on what actually takes place in the meeting? Does changing the name of the gathering eliminate denominationalism from their church practice? At best, we are dealing with mere titles and not the real substance of what the local church was designed to express. People may disagree with the idea that we go to different churches, however to change the word "church" does not alter the fact that they are still engaging in denominational behavior. It is not the title that we place on our meeting that sets us apart from denominational activity, but rather the revelation we have of the biblical "local church" and our obedience to rediscover how the biblical model is to form, as well as our rejection of all that contradicts it.

The reality is that we don't go to church any more than a child "goes to family." We don't teach our children that they must "go to their family" in order to be part of their family. We don't instill in our children the idea that being part of the family is something they can only attain to if they "go to" or "arrive at" their family." No! We instill within them the simple truth that they *are already part of the family*. Furthermore, we do not advocate the idea that family is a location which they must arrive at. We don't tell them to attend the family dinner in order to become part of the family. We get them to identify as being part of our family based upon the transcendent truth that they were *born* into the family, that they have the same DNA as the other members of the family, and that they are entitled to all of the benefits of that family by virtue of being part of the same bloodline. In the same way, we are part of the Church based upon Christ's DNA which was given to us, and therefore we can never again see the Church as an organization, a creed, a man-made entity, some building around the corner, or the product of human achievement.

Why does correct language even matter? Our language sums up what we believe, and if what we are saying is a reflection of what we believe, then our actions will prove whether or not we actually believe it. The truth is, many of us have not been taught some of the more profound and foundational truths in the New Covenant as they relate to the Church. And we may actually come to agree with the statement "we don't go to church, we are the church"; however if our greetings, our meetings, our teachings, and our entire involvement in spiritual fellowship still revolves around a location, a building, or some man-made organization, we are deceiving ourselves and remain in the sin of sectarianism – forming a local church outside of the biblical truths given to us in Scripture (we will explore the subject of sectarianism at greater length in chapters six and seven).

Jesus Revolutionizes the Location Worshippers

In John 4, Jesus engages in a remarkable conversation with a Samaritan woman who was collecting water from a well. She makes the statement, "Our fathers worshipped in this mountain; and ye say that in Jerusalem is the place where men ought to worship." Notice that the woman's understanding of worship shapes her question. She connects worship with a location. Some folks worship over here, and yet other folks worship over there. Jesus replies with, "The hour cometh, when ye shall neither in this mountain, nor yet at Jerusalem, worship the Father." He makes the startling statement that a time is coming when men will no longer regard worship to God in relation to a physical location. The Samaritan people were just as wrapped up into location-worship as the Jews were. They could not conceive of worshipping God outside of the temple, or of some holy sight. And Jesus came along saying that the hour had already come for this mindset to change. He goes on to say, "…But the hour cometh, and now is, when the true worshippers shall worship the Father in spirit and in truth: for the Father seeketh such to worship him." In Jesus' mind, "true worshippers" refers to those who can see the incarnational life of God not only in the person of Jesus Christ, but in themselves as well. Jesus was declaring that the time had come for man to see himself as having the very life of God within himself. The "location" for all future worship would be within man's heart and mind. In effect, He was transitioning mankind out from the mindset of temporary, physical, organizational religion into the true, eternal, transcendent, organismic communion between God and man.

> *God is not looking for location or geography, but people to be the vessel through which worship occurs*

With these bold statements to the Samaritan woman, Jesus was foreshadowing the true mindset for the Church. The expression of the Church's spirituality was not meant to be in connection to a physical building, structure, or organization. They would not be drawn to institutions or locations in order to worship, but would recognize that *true worship* is the worship that proceeds from within them. Peter called those who were part of the Church – God's temple. Paul referred to the Church as the temple of the Holy Spirit. The writer of Hebrews says that the tabernacle God has built was not built with human hands. And in Jesus' discourse with the woman at the well, He makes it clear that God is not looking for location or geography, but *people* to be the vessel through which worship occurs. In fact, the only form of worship which Jesus considered "true worship" was that which came forth from within the individual.

Organism vs. Organization

Once we recognize that Christ's Church is not some brick and mortar facility, but rather a living organism, we will begin to experience a truer more explosive expression of Christ, instead of the sterile worship that so often occurs in what we have wrongly called "churches," "houses of worship," and "fellowships." Once we are able to grasp our true nature as a *spiritual organism* rather than a *worldly organization*, we will be loosed both corporately and individually from all of the limitations that our man-made institutions have created for us. By saying "organization," we are not meaning that Christ's living organism called "The Church" is not organized, or that members of Christ's Body cannot organize meetings or messages. We are talking about molding the Body of Christ into the same kind of system that is common in almost every worldly business. This is a system that is created by man, and therefore must have man's fingerprint on all its affairs. By saying "organization" we are speaking of a man-made system of rules and regulations that place people in control of what goes on in every meeting, the order of our services, and the way each member will operate. Although the Body of Christ has organization within itself, it is not an organization that was started by a man, or needs man to maintain it; even as our physical bodies were designed to be organized apart from any action on our part, so is the Body of Christ made up of the divine life which comes from God and is sustained and operated by God alone.

As a spiritual organism, the Church is living, whereas an organization is not. As a spiritual organism, we are able to move, to grow, to involve ourselves in the affairs of the world around us according to the inherently divine ability within us; an organization cannot move, grow, or involve itself in the affairs of the world without the instrumentality of people. We have a conscience, the organization does not. We have within ourselves an effortless and eternal life that is perpetually living, whereas the organization is just an empty shell in need of organismic intervention. God did not create His Church in addition to many organizations; we *are* the very wineskin which God has poured Himself into, thus eliminating all other types and shadows of God's true dwelling place. We are a living organism, made up of living stones – a tabernacle that has not been made with human hands. We are the sum total of Christ's mystical Body in the earth who are the visible representation of the invisible life and presence of God. We are fully possessed by the life of Christ, and should never be mistaken for a worldly organization.

The Church was started by God, whereas an organization must be started by men. The Church does organize, however its identity is not found in what it organizes. We are a spiritually mystical organism which finds its creation and sustenance solely in the person of Christ. The Church consists of those who have realized their inclusion into the life, death, and resurrection of Jesus Christ. The Church is made up of those who have been recreated in Christ Jesus. The Church is God's workmanship, not man's invention. The Church is not dependent upon human methods, human organization, human intellects, or human ability to exist. The Church exists entirely in the person of Christ, as the expression of Christ in the earth. The Church is not dependent upon a physical location to exist, but rather was created as a spiritual reality, a transcendent entity, not needing anything within time and space to sustain its existence.

Chapter Five

Church Universal vs. Church Local

The Church is made up of people who do not find their identity in going to a structure, attending some organization, or rallying around groups that believe what they do on a set time each Sunday morning. They are a mystical Body of people who find their identity solely in Christ, who is their Head. This transcendent, eternal being called the Church is not bound by geography, but is as eternal and limitless as God Himself. Seeing this truth clearly will give us the correct foundation to begin revealing the only distinction made in Scripture concerning the Church of Christ – the *church universal* and the *church local*.

Universal Church

The universal church encompasses every believer in the world. We have brothers and sisters in Christ living in Asia, Africa, Russia, and Europe. They are just as much a part of the Church of Christ as we are in the U.S. We find the same common ground beneath all of us, whether it is the redemptive work of Christ on our behalf, the Pentecostal graces given by the Holy Spirit, or the hope in Christ's Second Coming. In Scripture, the universal church is always spoken of in the general sense. For example, Jesus says in Matthew 16:15, *"And I say also unto thee, That thou art Peter, and upon this rock I will build my church; and the gates of hell shall not prevail against it."* Here we find the Lord speaking of the Church He would build based upon a revelation of who He is. There was no mention of location or ethnicity in connection with Jesus' mention of the Church. Another example is in Ephesians 5:25 where Paul is giving this analogy, *"Husbands, love your wives, even as Christ also loved the church, and gave himself for it."* We know that Christ gave Himself for the entire Church – those members living in the U.S., Asia, Africa, Russia and Europe. Again, we find no specifications to where this Church would be

> *The universal church encompasses every believer in the world*

located or who would be included. In Colossians 1:18, Paul declares, *"And he is the head of the body, the church: who is the beginning, the firstborn from the dead; that in all things he might have the preeminence."* Notice that the only detail mentioned here is that all who are in the Church have the same Head – the person of Christ. In each of these verses, the common denominator is Christ – He is the foundation, the husband, and the head of the Church.

Now, although our brothers and sisters all over the world are part of the church universal, they are not part of the church local. We do not have personal fellowship with these people; we do not physically involve ourselves in their day-to-day activities. We cannot meet with those halfway across the world whenever we would like to discuss spiritual matters, partake together in meals, or lay hands on sick people within the community. We know that although Christ's Body is spread all throughout the world, we only experience the expression of that Body in the church local. And where is the church local? To gain a better understanding of this, we must look at the way in which all of the apostles spoke about the local church.

Local Church

Understanding that the church universal encompasses every believer in the world, and that there is a clear barrier to our personal fellowship with every believer, will help bring greater clarity as to the nature the local church. When studying everything that has been recorded for us in Scripture, it becomes evidently clear that *the local church is comprised of every believer within a geographical city.* And this distinction is made over and over again by the writers and apostles of the New Testament Church. With the exception of his letters to Philemon, Timothy, and Titus, all of the Apostle Paul's epistles were written to *cities*. He writes *"to all that be in Rome"* in his letter to the Romans. He writes *"To the church of God which is in Corinth"* in his letter to the Corinthians. He writes *"To the saints which are at Ephesus"* in his letter to the Ephesians. He writes *"to all the saints in Christ Jesus which are at Philippi"* in his letter to the Philippians. He writes *"To the saints and faithful brethren in Christ which are at Colossae"* in his letter to the Colossians. He writes *"unto the church of the Thessalonians which is in God the Father and in the Lord Jesus Christ"* in his letter to the

> *The local church is comprised of every believer within a geographical city*

Thessalonians. We know that after Paul's conversion, Barnabas brought him to the city of Antioch where *"A whole year they assembled themselves with the church, and taught much people. And the disciples were called Christians first in Antioch."* We see here that there was a church in Antioch. In each of these cases, believers were considered part of the local church in whichever city they lived.

In the Book of Acts, Luke writes that "There was a great persecution against the church which was at Jerusalem." Notice how he refers to Jerusalem as containing the church. He doesn't say that the persecution came against the "churches of Jerusalem" but that the persecution of Herod came against "the church." In his first epistle, the apostle Peter speaks of "the church that is at Babylon." Apparently, a local church had begun in the city of Babylon. (The revelation that the local church consists of every believe within a city is one of the most profound, especially when considering how big an impact it has on our understanding of sectarianism which crept into the early church, and is so rampant today. We will look at this in detail in chapters 6 and 7). In addition to Paul, Luke, and Peter, we find the Lord Jesus confirming the same truth that the local church is identified as every believer within a geographical city. In the second and third chapters of Revelation, Jesus reveals Himself as the principal of the Church. Notice how in each of the seven churches He encourages and rebukes, He mentions *cities*. He has no encouragement or rebuke for particular ministries or for particular ministers; He encourages the city of Ephesus, the city of Smyrna, the city of Pergamos, the city of Thyatira, the city of Sardis, the city of Philadelphia, and the city of Laodicea. These cities are called *churches.*

Not only is the local church identified with a city, but it is always spoken of in a singular tense. It is the "church of Rome" never the "churches of Rome." The only time we find the word "churches" employed is when the writer is speaking of some collective group of local churches, whether that is in many cities or in a province. Paul opens his letter to the Galatians by saying "Unto the *churches* of Galatia." Galatia was a province, which means that it contained *many cities*. And so, there were many local churches due to the fact that there were many cities. In Acts 15:41, we see Paul and Silas confirming the "churches" of Syria and Cilicia. Syria is a country with many cities, and Cilicia is a province with many cities. Again in Acts 16:4 we find this apostolic duo traveling "through the cities" seeing "the churches established in the faith." And again in 1 Corinthians 16:19 and 2 Corinthians 8:1 we discover that the continent of Asia and the province of Macedonia have many "churches" in each. In Galatians 1:22 we find Paul speaking of the *"churches of Judaea"* which are in Christ. Judaea was a Roman province and therefore contained many cities – each of which constituted a local church.

In all of the above examples, we see a clear pattern in the language used to convey the geographical city as being the expression of Christ's local church. In every continent there are many countries; in every country there are many provinces; and in every province there are many cities. The fact that there are many continents does not mean that there is such a thing as "continental churches," or some "mother church" that rules over all the other smaller churches within a continent. What we discover is that in every mention of a continent, for example Asia, we find the language "the *churches* of Asia." And in every mention of a country, for example Syria, we find the language "the *churches* of Syria." And in every mention of a province, for example Galatia, we find the language "the *churches* of Galatia." And yet, not once do we find any mention of the plural "churches" when dealing with a city. The reason is very simple: there is only *one* local church expression within a geographical city. And yet today, we have the idea of fellowships, congregations, houses of worship, and even home churches, as being legitimate local churches within our cities. The problem here is that there is no scriptural basis for the local church being relegated to a smaller unit then a geographical city. Once again, this distinction is of utmost importance if we are truly going to recapture the glorious unity that God intended for each of His local churches, while at the same time escaping the sin of division.

Church in the Home vs. Home Church

There are many today who assume that the few biblical mentions of church meetings in various homes, legitimizes starting a local church in someone's house. Many who are for the idea of "house churches" rightly assert that the Church of Christ is not bound to the four walls of the typical religious infrastructure that we have been accustomed to in the U.S. They are for the Church's liberation from institutional Christianity; however, they wrongly assert that the solution is to start "home churches" – making individual's homes the center for local churches. Although these passages do mention the Church as being in this home or that home, these mentions are simply stating that part of the local church within that given city was in someone's house.

Now, we know that the home *was* an instrumental meeting place for the local church, as is evident by Acts 2:46 where Luke states, "And they, continuing daily with one accord in the temple, and breaking bread from house to house, did eat their meat with gladness and singleness of heart," as well as in Acts 5:42 which says, "And daily in the temple, and in every house, they ceased not to teach and preach Jesus Christ," and in Acts 20:20 where Paul declares, "And how I kept back nothing that was profitable unto you, but have shewed you, and have taught you publicly, and from house to house." The apostle Paul, who called himself a "wise master builder" of the church, says in 1 Corinthians 16:19, "The churches of Asia salute you. Aquila and Priscilla salute you much in the Lord, with the church that is in their house." In his letter to Philemon, Paul opens his greeting by including Apphia and Archippus and "the church in thy house." In all five of these examples we find the functioning of Christ's Body occurring within various people's homes, and yet not once do we find a mention of Paul, Peter, or any of the other apostles starting churches in people's homes. Because the physical house is smaller than the scriptural definition for a local church – that being a geographical city – the house cannot be considered a local church. The local church may meet in a house, but the house itself is not the local church, nor are those who meet within a house considered a local church if there are other believers in that city. If you have believers in 10 locations around the city, they are all part of the same local church and cannot be considered as individual churches. It is not the physical structure or religious organization that determines a local church, but rather the geographical city which determines that particular local expression of Christ's Body.

More Than One

While it is true that just one person within a city can believe the Gospel and therefore find themselves included into Christ's redemptive work, it is also true that in order for that person to be part of a local church, he or she needs fellowship with at least one other believer. Since Scripture is clear on the grounds for a local church – a geographical city – and is equally as clear that the local church may have thousands of people within it (as seen in Acts 2 after Peter's Pentecostal speech), it needs at least two or three to be considered a local church. And although an individual may have the fullness of God's Spirit living within them, there is a manifest expression of Christ's Body when at least two people in a city believe the same Gospel. In fact, in order for Communion to take place as seen in 1 Corinthians 11, in order for spiritual graces to be shared as seen in 1 Corinthians 12 and 14, and in order for hands to be laid on those commissioned to preach abroad as seen in Acts 13, there must be at least two or three believers gathered in the same city.

When Paul went into a city that had never heard the Gospel, he preached until a church was established. But at what point was that local church established? It was not until at least two people believed his Gospel. When this happened, he left the city! In Acts 17, Paul travels to the Grecian city of Athens and preaches to the intelligencia on Mars Hill. Verses 32-34 state that "…when they heard of the resurrection of the dead, some mocked: and others said, We will hear thee again of this matter. So Paul departed from among them. Howbeit certain men clave unto him, and believed: among the which was Dionysius the Areopagite, and a woman named Damaris, and others with them." What is fascinating here is that soon after these "certain men" believed the Gospel, Paul leaves Athens! The very next verse is 18:1 which states that "After these things Paul departed from Athens, and came to Corinth." And what did Paul do in Corinth? He "found a certain Jew named Aquila, born in Pontus, lately come from Italy, with his wife Priscilla…And because he was of the same craft, he abode with them, and wrought: for by their occupation they were tentmakers. And he reasoned in the synagogue every Sabbath, and persuaded the Jews and the Greeks." Notice that once Paul made it to Corinth, he found a place where he could stay, obtained a job, and started preaching in the synagogues. This was the point of his apostolic mission – not merely to work or to develop new relationships – but to preach until there were at least two or three people who believed his Gospel.

Neither race, nor age, nor gender can be the bases for starting a local church. Furthermore, differences in doctrinal viewpoints cannot be the basis for starting a local church either. The cross of Christ effectively eliminated any carnal distinction between people and their particular beliefs on certain doctrines;

the cross eliminates all division between mankind, unifying him and giving him fellowship with His Creator and his fellow man. The point which we must see clearly is that *there is no smaller unit that a local church can fit into than that of a geographical city* – anything else is considered a sect, a denomination, or a heresy.

Chapter Six

Sectarianism Part I

In the first and third chapters of 1 Corinthians, the apostle Paul rebukes the church for having "contentions" and "divisions" among themselves, for having "envy," "strife," for being "carnal," and for "walking as men." And what produced this contention, division, envy, strife, carnality, and the tendency to walk as the rest of the world walks? We find the answer in a word – sectarianism. Merriam Webster defines the word *sect* as "a religious group that is a smaller part of a larger group and whose members all share similar beliefs."[1] The word "sect" is used five times in Scripture, however, the Greek translation of this word is used nine times. In Greek, the word "sect" is translated as "heresy." The Greek word is *hairesis*, and is mainly used to mean "dissensions arising from diversity of aims and opinions."[2] Now whereas opinions on Scripture may differ within a local city, the heresy is formed when those differing opinions lead individuals to break apart from one another, forming their own groups within that city. These groups are called "sects," or "heresies." Two of the most notable sects in the Jewish culture were the Pharisees and Sadducees. We know that the former believed in a resurrection of the dead, whereas the latter did not. Both of these groups consisted of Jews, however, due to their differing beliefs they formed their own distinct groups within their Judaistic religion. Like the Pharisees and Sadducees, there were those in the city of Corinth who began to form their own sects based upon the individual teachings of different personalities known to the early church. When we look at the twelfth verse of chapter one, we see four sects within the local church of Corinth. Some said "I am of Paul," others said "I am of Apollos," others said "I am of Cephas," and yet another group said "I am of Christ." Notice how three of the four sects revolved around apostles whereas the fourth revolved around Christ Himself. Paul flatly condemns *all* of these groups as sects.

Context for Sectarianism

In order to understand the context for a group of believers to be considered a sect, we must see the clear scriptural truth that a local church consists of every believer within a geographical city. Any group that forms under the banner of "local church" that is bigger than or smaller than a city is outside of the biblical outline for a local church. Corinth was such a city, which had a thriving group of believers birthed by apostolic preaching and demonstration. Over time, four groups arose which began to divide the local church into segments of thought. Instead of meeting in different locations within the city due to overcrowding in one area, they were meeting in different locations to *distance themselves from those who didn't believe quite like they did.* Whether we decide to form a group around some preacher, pastor, teacher, evangelist, apostle or prophet, or we decide to form a group around the person of Christ, any group that starts within a city that separates from other believers based upon differing beliefs is a sect. In fact, the only grounds which we have to physically separate from other believers within a city is if we do not have the physical space to accommodate those people.

> *Any group within a city which decides to create their own local church is dividing the local church*

Paul goes on to say, *"Is Christ divided? Was Paul crucified for you? Or were ye baptized in the name of Paul?"* The first part of this rhetorical question – "Is Christ divided?" – reveals the truth that any group within a city which decides to create their own local church is *dividing the local church*. As we discussed in chapter five, there are only two distinctions made when it comes to the Church of Christ: universal and local. Therefore the only division that stays within the scriptural guidelines is that division which exists between believers in one city and those believers who live across the world – whether they are in the city next to ours or the city in another country. There may be millions of local churches across the world but there can only be one within a city. This distinction was clear in Paul's mind, which is why he was bold enough to condemn the practice of sect-starting within the city of Corinth. The second part of the question – "Was Paul crucified for you? Or were you baptized in the name of Paul?" – reveals the apostle's distain and rejection for *personality worship* which has been prevalent since the dawn of the Church. Personality worship is a tendency of a worldly mindset which seeks to put man on a pedestal much like the Israelites did with Moses, Saul, and many others. God wanted His people to experience His presence, direction, and provision, but instead they rejected the notion of being led by God, and placed all of their desire for leadership upon a man. The church at Corinth was doing the same thing. They were basing their identity on the ministries of Paul, Apollos, and Peter, instead of seeing these ministries as single members of one local church.

Walking As Men

The apostle Paul uses the phrase "walking as men" to describe the Corinthian people in 1 Corinthians 3:3. By saying that the local church of Corinth was "walking as men," he was comparing them to the worldly man who is always trying to institutionalize life into some man-made system that ultimately becomes artificial, and separates itself from those who think and live differently. We see this clearly when considering the way a business is formed. When someone wants to starts a business, he or she must first have a product which meets some sort of need in the community. They then seek a way to advertise for it, with the goal of making their product and their business seem special, irreplaceable, and worth having. Next, they will obtain a building, make a sign, and create a system of management all to accommodate those who have need of their product. Whether it is a grocery store, post office, or a plumber's shop, each business has what the local person needs for his or her daily living. Each business has commonalities and meets individual needs of the community, however, each business remains divided based upon their individual specialty, individual profits, and individual ideas as it relates to the future of the organization. This is *not*, however, the way in which the local church was meant to conduct its affairs. The local church cannot be divided into compartments, separated by individual beliefs, or by individual ambitions. Furthermore, the local church cannot find its uniqueness in its advertising, its management, or its exterior image. The local church is the mystical Body of Christ within a local city, consisting of every believer in that geographical sphere. This is not the simplified or slanted version of the local church – this is *the only version of the local church in Scripture.*

Members of the Institution vs. Members of Christ's Body

When we speak of "sectarianism," we are also speaking of "institutionalism," which is the inevitable consequence of breaking off into sects. By "institutionalism" we are talking about that sectarian mindset which views the local church like a worldly institution. The institutional church is that organized, money-based, sectarian-type group which forms, utilizing some building space in order to set up a highly personalized organization with a CEO – the pastor – and a hierarchy that includes assistant pastors, evangelists, worship teams, and a whole list of programmatic systems which are set in place to try and provide everything that the average believer might need to meet his or her spiritual and natural desires. The sectarian mind sees the institution as the context for all of the biblical ideas about the local church. For example, since an institution is considered to be the local church, it must have an apostle, prophet, evangelist, pastor and teacher operating within for it to be considered a "true" local church. And, there must be programs to meet the needs of those who feel called to various ministries, whether that is hospitality, children's ministry, evangelism, or music ministry. The institutional church becomes the illegitimate miniature version of the local church described in scripture.

The problem with institutionalism is that we inevitably see the "joint of supply" which Paul speaks of as coming exclusively from those within our own institution. We thereby disconnect ourselves from the rest of the local church who has also been called to supply our needs. Since our belief that the local church consists of every believer within our particular institutions rather than in the whole city, we have effectively hindered the growth of Christ's Body in that city. Also, by seeing the local church as the institution which we attend each Sunday, we have damaged our belief system in so many other ways, mainly by trying to fit all of Christ's members and all of Christ's manifestations into our little groups. The result is that our leadership teams place the weight of responsibility on our shoulders to do what only the entire Body in that city can do, along with creating the false mindset that we are self-sufficient as a local group of people, not needing the help of our brothers and sisters down the road. The truth is, there are members of His Body that live across the street from us who have tremendous spiritual encouragement for us; however, since they do not attend our particular institution, we live week after week missing that powerful supply of Christ's Spirit.

> *The only qualification for people to become members of the local church – whether or not Christ has received them*

In 1 Corinthians 12:27, the apostle Paul states "Now ye are the body of Christ and members in particular." From this verse we can see our membership as not being found in our commitment to some man-made institution. The fact that we have "membership classes" reveals the sectarian thread that has woven itself into the fabric of the local church. Since each sect is formed by individuals within a local city, and is set up like a worldly institution, there is a need for artificial membership in the same way that we would need membership for a gym, a country club, or a specialty store. Romans 15:7 declares, *"Wherefore receive ye one another, as Christ also received us to the glory of God."* Here we see the only qualification for people to become members of the local church – whether or not Christ has received them. We find no talk of creating membership classes within the Church of Jerusalem, nor in the Church of Rome. We do not see the apostles gathering together and discussing qualifications for people to become members of Christ's Body.

One of the main reasons we have adopted the idea of membership in the Church is because through membership classes, we are able to screen those who desire to be a part of our organizations. We will give them four weeks, or four months, or four years of teaching in order for them to be qualified to serve our organization, or minister in the front of the congregation, or pray for the sick. We have created a system where we can regulate who can minister and who cannot, all in the name of "knowing those who labor among us." The truth is, this verse found in 1 Thessalonians 5:12 is not saying that we are to know those *in order that they may* labor among us, but that we ought to know those *who are* laboring among us. We cannot keep people from ministry simply because we don't know them, or because we may not agree with everything they believe, or because we do not feel they are mature enough to minister. All of these ideas are based upon the error that *people* can begin a ministry, or are responsible to start and stop other people's ministries. No! We are *all* members of Christ's Body and He alone is the Head.

Rallying Around Personalities

Like the people in the city of Corinth, we are plagued with people-worship in our present church culture. We perceive certain gifts within different members of Christ's Body and we seek to exalt them in the same way that the Israelites wanted to exalt Saul as their king. In exalting personalities, we have wandered into sectarianism. We say, "This person is more prophetic, therefore I will follow him because he is like me," or "This person is more evangelistic, therefore I will follow her because she seems to be most qualified," or "This person is more of a teacher, therefore I will follow him because I respect his ministry the most." We follow those who are like us, or we follow those who believe like we do. We say, "I will be a part of this person's ministry because they teach things that are in line with what I believe." Instead of seeing each person within a local city as part of the local church, we attempt to divide Christ's Body according to preferences. "Well, I just prefer teaching on Jewish rituals." And so, we follow the person who emphasizes Jewish rituals in their ministry. The reality is that we *are* and *should be* influenced by prophets, pastors, and teachers; however *we are not* supposed to be led around by people in the New Covenant, the way in which those under the Old were led about. Under the Old Covenant, mankind had no conscious awareness of an indwelling Spirit as we should. Under the Old Covenant, mankind was not capable of living with any kind of sustained direction for their lives. The Israelites needed to be led by the hand like children because they stubbornly refused the leadership which God wanted to personally give them. We do not live under the Old Covenant anymore, and have been made aware that God is dwelling within us, and desires to be our sole head and our sole director. Only when we see God as having taken the helm of our spiritual and natural lives can we see the error of being led by men.

Starting Ministries vs. Ministry of the Holy Spirit

When we become fully convinced that all ministry is sourced in and flows by the operation of God's Spirit within each of us, we will be able to throw off the false idea that we are capable of "starting ministries." And when we throw off the idea that we are capable of "starting ministries" we will eliminate yet another form of sectarianism within the local church. First, we must understand what a "ministry" is, where and how it originates. Nowhere in Scripture are we told that a man has the ability to "start a ministry." We find no mention of Paul starting his own apostolic ministry, of Philip starting his own evangelistic ministry, or of Apollos starting his own teaching ministry. And yet, we know that Paul was considered an apostle, Philip was considered an evangelist, and Apollos was considered a teacher. We also find no mention of ministers filling out paperwork to begin their ministries, deciding at what time they would start their ministries, or attempting to get fellow Christians to join their ministries. In Acts 20:24, the apostle Paul says, "But none of these things move me, neither count I my life dear unto myself, so that I might finish my course with joy, and the ministry, which I have received of the Lord Jesus, to testify the gospel of the grace of God." Notice here that Paul received his ministry "of the Lord Jesus." In 2 Corinthians 5:18, Paul says, "And all things are of God, who hath reconciled us to himself by Jesus Christ, and hath given to us the ministry of reconciliation." Again, he makes the claim that we all have been given a ministry "by Jesus Christ." In Colossians 4:17, Paul says "And say to Archippus, Take heed to the ministry which thou hast received in the Lord, that thou fulfil it." Once again, he states that a fellow worker for the Gospel received his ministry "in the Lord." And lastly, Paul says in 1 Timothy 1:12, "And I thank Christ Jesus our Lord, who hath enabled me, for that he counted me faithful, putting me into the ministry." It was Jesus Christ who put Paul into the ministry.

When people take it upon themselves to "start a ministry," they are unknowingly in the beginning stages of sectarianism. If we entertain the idea that a "ministry" is something to start, we must ask ourselves, "where did this ministry come from?" And if this ministry came from God, then what are we actually "starting"? If God has given us a ministry of evangelism, what left is there for us to "start"? We may be clued into the fact that we have been called as evangelists, but do we need the government to recognize that in order to make it official? Do we need the Church to recognize it to make it official? Do we need *any* human agency to make our ministry official? The answer is

> *We do not need anything or anyone to make the ministries we possess, legitimate and functional*

unequivocally NO! The point here is that the act of trying to make our ministries *official* typically involves advertising for it, getting financial support, being sanctioned by an institution, and promoting it like a business. However, we do not need *anything* or *anyone* to make the ministries we possess, legitimate and functional.

Disagreements vs. Sectarianism

Many people mistake disagreements over doctrinal issues for sectarianism. For example, one person may see the work of Christ on the Cross as having completely taken away the old nature from man, once and for all. Another person may see the same work of Christ as having made the possibility for that old nature to be taken away, but that each person must do something to destroy that nature in his or her own life. These two perspectives may bring two people to the point of debate, perhaps causing the circle of debate to grow as others are brought into the conversation, mainly in order to hammer out what the Scripture actually says. However, this disagreement, for however long it stays a disagreement, is not heresy. It *is* a division in the sense that there are two divided thoughts on the same issue, however, it is not the kind of division that Paul condemns when he says "there is among you envying, and strife, and divisions." Again, the reasoning over doctrine along with disagreements over ideas does not constitute a sect. Only when those in disagreement to one another form their own groups around their particular beliefs do we see the sin of sectarianism at work. Consider the local church of Jerusalem. There was a division in thought around the idea of Gentiles becoming believers (see Acts 15). Some of the Jews believed that these newly converted Gentiles should be circumcised whereas others believed that circumcision was not to be included into the Gospel of Christ for the New Covenant believer.

We've become so accustomed to the idea that "division" is a bad thing. However, what most of us call "division" is nothing more than people believing differently about the Gospel. And yet, we find the apostle Paul stating in the fourth chapter of Ephesians that apostles, prophets, evangelists, pastors and teachers exist to cause the "unity of the faith" amongst the local churches – literally meaning *that we all believe the same thing*. Obviously, we don't all believe the same thing. The corporate Body of Christ is not yet fully mature. This immaturity does not mean that we are sinning, but rather that we have not been informed or convinced of the true Gospel.

The truth is that everything we do is the result of some form of division. We go to one store over the next because we have divided each's goods in our minds and have made decision on what would best meet our needs. We make divisions over foods based upon what is good for our body. We make divisions in our relationships to determine who is best suited to be in specific roles in our lives. In addition, when it comes to theology, we have also made divisions over what we believe is true and what we believe is not true. In order to come to the truth about any one doctrine or idea, we must settle it in our minds that not all division is wrong. Jesus said he came to bring division. Was Jesus wrong to say this? Paul said that we are to rightly divide the word. Was Paul in error to teach that we are to divide what we read and hear? *The truth is that division is only sin when in the context of sectarianism.* This is the only place in the New Testament where you see the word "division" as being sin. We may disagree on doctrinal issues, but we must never form our own groups based upon our doctrinal persuasions. And yet, some will say "How can I fellowship with another person who doesn't believe exactly as I do?" This is where we need to see our brothers and sisters through the lens of Christ's finished work. We are all maturing in our belief systems, and yet, we are already mature in Christ. We are growing in our knowledge of all that God has done through Christ, and yet we are every bit as perfect as God has said we are. It is the paradox of being perfect in Christ, and yet maturing in our understanding of that perfection. While in the maturing process, we must bear with one another, and never say "I have no need of you."

Some may say, "Why don't we all just get along? Why do we need to split hairs over the definition of church? Why can't we just keep meeting in our organized ministries and love one another? Why do we have to cause more division in the body of Christ by telling people they need to come out of the institutions? What does it matter if we have many local churches within a geographical city?" And then there are some people who will rightly say that the building is *not* the Church. They will attest to the fact that the institution is a sect and that the Church of Christ exists apart from whatever sectarian gathering they still attend. However, when told that Christ requires their maturity, and therefore their separation from the institution, they are offended and will often times defend that very institution. Their offense betrays their original consent that they are the Church apart from their institution – their identity becomes confused. They are actually saying that they are the Church apart from their sect, *and* that their sect is needed to identify them as the Church, however, *both cannot be true*. The distinction between the church universal, the church local, and the many sects within our cities may seem like an insignificant one, however according to the New Covenant, the apostle Paul, and the Lord Jesus Christ, it is of utmost importance. And although there are many adjustments we need to make in our thinking if we are going to become mature sons and daughters, understanding sectarianism and doing what we can to eliminate this sin will bring greater manifestations of unity in the local church then we have seen in our lifetime.

Chapter Seven

Sectarianism Part II

In light of seeing the truth that our institutions, man-made ministries, and hierarchical human ranks are unscriptural, and breed ungodly division in Christ's local church, we must take steps to eliminate such carnal interference. In his book *The Normal Christian Church Life*, the Chinese apostle Watchman Nee speaks of these divisions as fences. Many are content to just shake hands over the fences, but few are willing to tear those fences down. Why are people afraid to tear down these sectarian fences which we have tolerated for centuries? For starters, many people are simply ignorant to these truths. We have not heard too much teaching on Paul's rebuke to the Corinthians for personality worship, sectarianism, and carnal behavior as it relates to organization-starting. We have trusted that our institutional leaders know what's best for us, and have not dared stray outside the theological lines that have been set before us, week after week. It is true that we have had our eyes peeled for such sins as adultery, mismanaging money, and anger, but do we really understand how diabolical sectarianism is? Furthermore, many pastors have such a big stake in their institutions – they've literally built their lives and the lives of countless others around their particular organizations. Since each of these sects run like a business, some of which have tens of thousands of dollars each month coming in from eager parishioners, it is especially difficult to just wrap up the entire operation. Still, at some point, we must allow the true revelation of Christ's local church to revolutionize the way we meet together, express our individual and corporate identities, and demonstrate our love to the world.

Sectarianism – A Work of the Flesh

Like all sins of the flesh, we do not overcome them by *trying* to overcome them; we must see how Christ has overcome them for us. Sectarianism – the act of forming groups around our particular belief systems, separating ourselves from others, and creating "local churches" that are smaller than, or bigger than, the geographical boundaries of a city – has been dealt with in the universal church sense and in the local church sense. The former is found in Ephesians 2:14-15 which says *"For he is our peace, who hath made both one, and hath broken down the middle wall of partition between us; Having abolished in his flesh the enmity, even the law of commandments contained in ordinances;*

for to make in himself of twain one new man, so making peace." Here we see that the ministry of Jesus Christ removed the middle wall of separation between us and God. We have been gloriously liberated from the idea of separation from the presence of Christ, and have come to recognize that *nothing* can separate us from His divine love. Also, we have been freed from the false idea that our lives are our own – we have been made a part of the Godhead, filled with the divine life. Not only are we a part of God's divine nature and are in complete union with Christ, but we share our divine nature with every part of Christ's Body, being in complete unity with every believer around the world. This is what we mean by the fact that sectarianism has been dealt with in the *universal church* sense.

Now, just as Christ eliminated all separation between man and God, and unified us with every believer around the world, He has also eliminated all separations between us and our brothers and sisters in our individual cities. First, we must truly see that the sin of sectarianism is in fact a work of the flesh. Galatians 5:19-20 says "Now the works of the flesh are manifest, which are these; Adultery, fornication, uncleanness, lasciviousness, Idolatry, witchcraft, hatred, variance, emulations, wrath, strife, seditions, *heresies…*" Notice that the word "heresies" is mentioned at the end of this long list of "works of the flesh." The word "heresies" is the Greek word *hairesis* meaning "the act of taking, capture; choosing or choice; that which is chosen; a body of men following their own tenets/sect or party i.e. Sadducees, Pharisees, Christians; dissensions arising from diversity of opinions or aims." The Church today has no problem protesting abortion, warning about adultery, or preaching against any of the other more visible sins in our communities. We do this because we believe that these are sins which ultimately hurt the collective conscience and spiritual state of those we know and love. And yet, when it comes to sectarianism – the "heresies" mentioned in Galatians 5:20 – we have allowed our strong, traditional background in it to make us feel as though it were an optional thing to correct, or we haven't seen the reality of heresy in our local cities. Galatians 5:24 gives us the truth about the sin of heresy. Paul says, *"And they that are Christ's have crucified the flesh with the affections and lusts."* According to verse 20 and 24, Paul is clear here that the "flesh" and its "affections and lusts" includes the sin of heresy, which is by definition the sin of sectarianism. This tendency to form parties around particular beliefs, thereby separating from others who believe differently, has been dealt with by Jesus Christ as well. There should be no more room in our Christianity for this fleshly sin, especially as Christ has already nailed it to His cross. This is what we mean by the fact that sectarianism has been dealt with in the *local church* sense.

Misguided Sympathies

Many of us may still have deep sympathies toward the various sects of which we have been a part. It is difficult to contemplate that our traditional upbringings have included such a gross error, and even more difficult to go a step further and eliminate such an error. In our present institutional gatherings, it would be helpful for us to ask the question, "What was the origin of the group that I am part of who gather in this way?" In the Church today, we have been so conditioned to think of churches forming as the result of human effort. However, based on what we know in the Book of Acts, we find *no* case of anyone "starting a ministry," "starting an organization," or "starting a church" for that matter. The transition between a particular city being full of unbelievers, and having the beginnings of a local church was a seamless one. There was a silent awakening which was produced by apostolic preaching that did not have the noise of man's institutional machinery drumming up parishioners. We see the preaching of the Gospel, the coming together of those who believed – mainly in homes – and the establishing of each member as they had been gifted and set in the Body by the will of God. Why didn't Paul start "Paul's Apostolic Ministries International" and call unto himself those who wanted to receive apostolic training? Why didn't Peter set up "Peter's Apostolic Mission to Jerusalem" after he had preached in the streets of the city? Why didn't Philip set up "Philip's International School of Evangelism" in Samaria after he had preached and seen a city-wide revival? Why didn't Jesus tell His disciples to set up "schools of ministry," or "hubs of revival," or "centers for eager parishioners desiring to better themselves in their unique anointings?" The reason is simple. *God's wisdom excludes the very notion that man has the ability to start a church or begin a ministry.* God's wisdom causes all the focus of the Church to be on Christ, whereas man's wisdom causes the focus of the Church to be split – half on Christ and half on the institutional leadership. God's wisdom preaches the equality of all Christ's members, whereas man's wisdom exalts some members over others based upon talent, personality, and academic degrees. God's wisdom reveals the Church as a spiritual entity, not needing any human ingenuity to prosper or continue, whereas man's wisdom reveals the Church as a human organization, needing constant human commitment, personality, and money to survive.

Why So Much Difficulty?

There are many people who are beginning to see the error of having sects within our cities, and yet find it difficult to remove themselves from this sin altogether. In fact, there are

> *God's wisdom excludes the very notion that man has the ability to start a church or begin a ministry*

several justifications for continuing these sects. We experience a degree of fellowship with our brothers and sisters each week. Since we are commanded to continue in our fellowship with each other, we see the institution as facilitating that need. We experience a degree of Body-ministry in our particular groups, whether that is through the laying on of hands, some form of musical presentation, or by being able to express such spiritual graces as prophecy, tongues, words of knowledge, or the working of miracles. We experience a degree of evangelism in our organizations as there are often outreaches available for eager participants. We experience a degree of leadership as we are being taught each week by a few central figures. We experience a degree of material support, as there may be collections taken for specific needs that we or our families may have. We experience a degree of acceptance as we are greeted warmly as we enter the building, and may even be invited to some form of dinner if we are new to that particular institution. And beneath a long list of reasons that we may stay involved in our sects, we have been ignorant to the original design for Christ's local church. It is clear that, although there have been times we have been helped in our institutions – whether spiritually, financially, or physically – we cannot use this to justify our continued involvement. Whereas we may have been helped in differing degrees, once we become enlightened to the truth about the local church, staying involved will serve only to keep us immature. If the sect is sinful, it must be removed. The local church is not hindered by this removal, but rather is liberated to function free of the rigid control that has been imposed on it for centuries.

As far as the current institutional leadership goes, there are many fears that might prevent them from dismantling their sects. Some might believe that they will lose their personal impact in their city, others that they will somehow lose their influence with people. There may also be the fear that they will lose their purpose in life, and that the local church will be void of real leadership. The root of the fear that a minister will lose his or her personal impact in their city is found in the fact that they built their organization, and assumed that *they* were responsible for changing their city. In their minds, the burden of transforming the city rests on their shoulders, as opposed to on the shoulders of Christ's collective Body in that region. Institutionalism has a way of blinding the individual to all the other believers that are living and functioning as Christ's members in the rest of the city. Regarding losing their influence with the people they have gathered in their organization, this is a fear that is based upon the false notion that *they* are the heads of Christ's local church, when in actuality it is *Christ* who is the head of the local church. As far as losing their purpose in life, this is a fear based in the misconception that their identities are unalterably linked to the organization they have built. However, the identity of the individual– regardless of their calling – rests securely in Christ and is not based upon our successes in organization building. And lastly, the idea that the local church will be void of real leadership if the institutions are removed is a result of seeing institutional leadership as the *only* kind of leadership that exists. This mindset has been molded by centuries of the Church accepting sectarian leadership. However, New Covenant, apostolic leadership is not based upon a person's ability to start an organization, but rather on that person's spiritual maturity and calling to become a leader within a city of believers (We will study this more in Volume II).

The very idea of dismantling a particular sect is often quickly dismissed by those who are in current leadership simply because the alternative to meeting in this way is so hard for them to accept. Many are fearful of losing control over what they've known all their lives. Others will devise a more detailed objection of dismantling their institutions, citing verses that point to Christian leadership, or submitting to elders, or the fact that there is a gift of administration, or that there are some ministries like the apostle and prophet that appear to be on the front lines more than others. Whereas there is order, different administrations, and leadership in the local church, none of these truths can validate the starting or maintaining of a sect within the local church – whether that involves rallying around one personality or setting up the church like a worldly organization.

Should We Reform the Institution?

There are still others who have a deeper understanding of the problems within our institutional churches, who are trying to reform them. They see the immaturity of members when it comes to doctrine, the lack of understanding when it comes to identity, and the unscriptural dependence upon the pastor to be the director of Christ's local church. They will point to Martin Luther as their example – the 16th century reformer whose desire to reform the Catholic Church spawned a massive exodus from that institution. Luther had a revelation of scripture that had been lost throughout the centuries, namely that we have been saved by grace through faith, and that the entirety of Christ's Church has been called as priests to serve in Christ's kingdom. He saw many other evils being practiced by the Catholic priests of the day, which inspired him to write the famous *95 Theses* which he later nailed to the door of the Castle Church of Wittenberg. Making good use of the Guttenberg printing press, Luther translated the Bible into the language of the common man in Germany. The result of his boldness to reform Catholic doctrine was that the people's mindset shifted, and they discovered a new-found freedom to search the scriptures for themselves. Along with this freedom came the ability to meet with other believers in non-Catholic type settings – whether that was in homes or in rented buildings. The problem was that, whereas Luther had a great revelation of Scripture, he did not have an understanding of sectarianism. In fact, his goal was never to start a *Lutheran Church*, but to reform the Catholic Church. In other words, he was not concerned with eliminating the great sect of Catholicism as much as he was about changing the way Catholics thought about Scripture. Now, there was an inevitable break from the Catholic Church, however many of those who broke away did what so many have done throughout history – they formed an entirely new sect by calling themselves "Lutherans." For all the good that came out of Luther's reformation, the sin of sectarianism just disguised itself with a new name and a new set of beliefs nailed onto Christ's Church. This movement would develop with new leadership and new doctrine, all the while maintaining the same error of the Roman Catholic Church – sectarianism.

And so, there are those today who see the problems with sectarian church organizations, and will attempt to do what Luther did – reform the organization. While it is true that the Church today needs a reformation, we need something more than just reforming individual sects; first we need a reformation in our belief system as it relates to the local and universal churches, and then an awareness that we must function as believers completely free of the man-made divisions that plague our cities. Our need is not only for teaching on sectarian-free church life; we need the demonstration of that life. It will take individuals who become convinced of the Scriptures' clear ban on *all* forms of party-spirit, factional, sectarian, institutional, man-made, man-focused ministry endeavors, along with the revelation of how the local church is supposed to be established, and how each member is called to function within the geographical boundaries of their respective city.

Only when we have the correct understanding of the biblical Church, the mind of God concerning His ministers, and the way we are to establish people in the faith, can we do the work God has called us to do without falling into the trap of sectarianism. The heart of the person who truly understands the sin of sectarianism, and is willing to do whatever it takes to eliminate it in his or her life, will be most useful to the Lord in helping others see how we are intended to meet together and function as Christ's Body. The people who truly understand the biblical Church will not seek to put their name on the ministry, set up some ministry institution, collect money to further their own particular ministerial agenda, or make the rest of the Church feel subservient to them. We see clear leadership in the Church of Paul's day, clear instruction, clear authority, and clear ambition as to the preaching of the Gospel and the establishing of churches. However, we see parallel to this, a great emphasis on removing the idea that the instruction, authority, ambition, and establishing of churches has *anything* to do with establishing some man's ministry, some man's ambition, some man's authority, and some man's instruction. We may better understand the distinction between the person who has the correct understanding of establishing the local church, and the one who does not, by using the example of two men.

Larry & Steve

Two men are traveling to the same city. The first man we will call Larry and the second we will call Steve. Larry represents the sectarian-minded minister, whereas Steve represents the non-sectarian-minded minister. When they arrive into the city, they both go to work preaching the Gospel. Larry finds 5 individuals who believe his message. He instructs his group, reinforcing the idea that he is their pastor. He lays out a plan that includes all 5 of his followers to give money each week to help them get a building where they all can continue in the ministry. Larry has a genuine concern for each of his followers, and seeks to help each of them develop their own abilities. Over time, they are able to raise enough money to secure a building down town. Having finally secured a building, Larry formulates a name for the ministry – "The Church of This City." He legalizes this name by obtaining a non-profit status such as the

501c3, and continues as the ministry's CEO. More people begin to see the building's sign and begin congregating each week with Larry and his initial 5 members. Through word of mouth the congregation grows to 100 people. They begin to find musical people to play songs during the service, as well as volunteers to help with the children. Larry greets the people with "I am so glad you are fellowshipping with *our* church." He goes on to say "We would love for you to fill out membership forms so that you can be a member of *our* church." There is an overtly exclusive and possessive tone to what Larry says when he talks to people about the church. He uses words like "mine" and "our" when describing his group of believers. After about 2 years, Larry has grown his group from 100 to 300, has developed a rapport in the city as a "growing church," has developed an outreach program, a music ministry, and a multi-dimensional leadership team that consists of elders and deacons. Since Larry has set himself up as this group's pastor, he takes out a salary from the money collected each week. He doesn't work a job in the world for he sees his pastoral ministry as his calling. His meetings are all planned ahead of time, with a certain number of songs prepared by the worship team to start every meeting, a short time to greet the people after the music is over, an offering teaching to precede the collection of money, and a sermon prepared that week for the people. After the sermon, there is a time when people can move from their rowed seating to the front of the building where the "alter" is, so that they can receive prayer from a select group of people who have been with Larry for a while. After all of this is done, everyone is dismissed. Larry's goal is to grow "The Church of This City" in the name of "having an even greater impact on the city," and "to eventually impact other countries."

On the other hand, we have Steve who finds 5 individuals believing his message, and begin meeting in his home. Steve has a real concern about each of the people that come to his house, and begins to teach them the Gospel. As each week passes, the members are being convinced that *they* have become the house of God, that *they* are the building of the Holy Spirit, and that *they* are filled with the divine nature of Christ. Instead of raising money for a physical building, they are encouraged to give each week into a collective fund where money is saved in an account and only used when someone within the group has some form of material need. This way, no one within the group will lack. Since Steve does not see a scriptural basis for collecting a salary from the local church, he works a job the rest of the week to provide for his own needs. Through word of mouth, the group grows from 5 to 20 people in the first couple of months. Since space in his house is limited, and cannot fully accommodate 20 people, he has 12 of the people meet in his home, while the other 8 meet in the home of a more spiritually mature brother who can facilitate meetings. Steve does not see a scriptural basis for centralizing the local church into one building, but sees the biblical pattern of meeting house to house. In so doing, he effectively raises someone else up to do the work of pastoring yet another group of believers. As more homes are opened for meetings, money is still collected from each group and placed into the central fund so that more and more needs within each group can be met. Like in Acts 2, everyone gives and no one has lack. Steve refrains from using exclusive and possessive terms when referring to the group of believers that are meeting; instead, he speaks of the local church that is forming as Christ's Body, Christ's members, and Christ's Church. The contents of each meeting consist of music, teaching, opportunities to minister in the nine graces described in 1 Corinthians 12 and 14, and fellowship with food and interaction. Although Steve is acting as a pastor over his group, he is not centralizing the focus on himself, but rather is continually encouraging those attending to use their gifts, all the while demonstrating that it is the Holy Spirit who wills through each person, and will never interrupt Himself. Steve is not overly concerned with controlling the meetings, or making them carbon-copied from the previous week's meeting. The music does not *have* to come first, and the teaching does not *have* to come last. As each group grows to each home's maximum capacity, another home opens up, until there are groups meeting all across the city. Each group has an understanding that they are *all* part of the same local church, and that there are no divisions amongst them, even though they are meeting in separate places due to limited space. Since the message that each person hears reveals that they are already members of Christ's Body, there is no need for membership classes, or for some kind of initiation into an institution. Also, whether people are new believers or mature believers, they are *all* given an opportunity to minister, as each one has the same Spirit within them. Most of all, the meetings that Steve has initiated are known for their *spontaneity*. Everything is done according to the will of the Spirit, not some preset order which is so common in Larry's institutional setting. Steve is not concerned with trying to grow a ministry to impact the country or the nations of the world, but is steadfast in his commitment to see the local church of his city come to maturity, knowing that it is the Holy Spirit's job to send out apostles or prophets or evangelists as He wills.

From these two examples, we see a common denominator – both Larry and Steve are part of Christ's Church, and everyone who becomes a believer is part of the local church of that city. What differs is the revelation that both of these men have. One believes that there is a need to institutionalize the local church, while the other believes that it is unnecessary and unbiblical to institutionalize the local church. Larry has made his ministry his profession, and in so doing, the entire operation runs like a professional business, from the finances to the décor of the building, to the sign out front, and the predictable program that is followed each week. Steve, on the other hand, has no need to build up his ministry, but rather to use his ministry to build the local church. Consequently, he leaves room for the Holy Spirit to set the order of each meeting, and has eliminated unnecessary financial overhead that is in keeping with acquiring and maintaining a building. Larry's effort revolves around his particular vision for the organization he has started. As a result, the people in his group speak of him like the Israelites spoke of Moses – "Pastor Larry is the visionary. Pastor Larry is our leader. Pastor Larry is the man of God. Pastor Larry must approve if we are to move forward in this or that endeavor." Steve's effort revolves around preaching, teaching and demonstrating the Gospel to the point that those who hear and experience the Gospel begin to see themselves as fully possessing the divine life of Christ. The result is that Steve is not exalted as "The Pastor" but is seen as another brother – perhaps an elder, more mature brother – but as possessing the same divine nature. Larry encourages people to see the pecking order within the institutional church, believing that his role is more important than the other roles, and that without him, people will not function properly. Steve encourages people to see the eternal value of an eternal God living within them, and that even if he is not present, they have everything they need to function as a member of Christ's Body.

At the end of the day, we will either allow our minds to be transformed by these New Covenant truths concerning the Church, or we will allow our traditions to stop us from entering into true fellowship with one another. If the objections to the idea of sectarianism as laid out in this chapter are that "we already have a system that works," or "we have never heard of this," or "I don't think that's what the Bible is really saying," then the one objecting needs to be able to defend the systems and institutions they are a part of from a biblical perspective. Otherwise, they will be found in the same error of all those groups that have used extra-biblical information to mold their church experience and determine their way of worship. However, if we become convinced of the deception that sectarianism has laid upon us – the way in which it keeps us divided, the way in which it keeps us immature, and the way in which it turns the Church of Christ into a business of the world – we must leave it altogether, and trust the Holy Spirit to guide us back into God's original design for the local church.

Chapter Eight

The Church Meeting Part I

The greatest reflection of Christ's glory is found in His Church. There is no greater representation of His perfection, His power, and His life than in the hearts and minds of his saints. When His members come together within a city there is an exponential outpouring of divine glory that spills forth from each person. A communion is experienced amongst them that is sweeter than any other earthly pleasure. The plans and purposes of God are revealed for the cities in which they meet, and the impact of the local churches becomes recognized and often feared by natural governments. In each meeting, there is a heavenly aura, an eternally blissful emotion, and a satisfying unity that is experienced by the people. There is a plurality of ministry that occurs during each gathering which edifies the group, brings clarity to confused minds, bolsters the individual's

Christ-like identity, and empowers each member to fulfill their destiny.

For many, these attributes of the local church meeting are spoken of as either the ideal, or as if they were already happening. And yet, the truth is that we are not seeing this reality in our sectarian services. The kind of equality in ministry that Paul teaches to the local churches of Corinth and Ephesus is hard to reconcile with today's top-down, hierarchical, business-like class system, where attendees have to jump through institutional hoops, impress leadership with their devotion, or commit to a group for several months before being able to express who they are in Christ. The simplicity of ministering "as the Spirit wills" has been replaced by ministry as the pastor wills. The creativity and spontaneity of being led by the Spirit has been stifled by a programmatic system of pre-planned events. The question we must ask is, "Why is this the present reality for most of us?" The truth is that the Church meeting today does not differ much from the Jewish gatherings in the temple, under the Old Covenant. Seeing the biblical distinction between the meeting of the Israelites in the temple, and the meeting of Christ's Church under the New Covenant, is key if we are to experience the complete liberty of the biblical Church meeting.

The Meeting Place of the Jews

Before the Church, the Crucifixion, and the Incarnation of the Messiah, the Jews understood that gathering together in the synagogue was necessary in order to fulfill their religious duties, as well as to fellowship with other Jews. The physical structure in which they met held great meaning to the Jewish mind, as it was under the leadership of Moses that the Israelites first constructed a tent to represent the place of God's presence. This tent would be set up for Moses to "meet" with the Lord, and receive instruction on how and where to lead the people. Surrounding the tent was a court which consisted of ceremonial and symbolic washings and offerings performed by the Levitical priests. Within the tent there were two main sections: the first was called the *Holy Place*, the second was called the *Most Holy Place*. In the midst of the outer courts, the Holy Place, and the Most Holy Place, there was a host of different rituals, as well as a highly detailed décor plan to bring out specific colors, woods, precious metals, and aesthetic accents that all pointed toward something else. Everything that Moses was instructed to build was to foreshadow the spiritual building that Christ would create over a thousand years later.

Several centuries after the tabernacle of Moses was built, King Solomon was tasked with building a temple that would accentuate the kind of spiritual interaction which Moses established. For the Israelites, the temple was the central place for worship and sacrifice to God. Just like in the tent, there was a plethora of symbolic décor that was all to foreshadow something else – namely the Messianic appearance of Christ. As other nations came to fight and ultimately conquer Israel, the temple was often renovated or destroyed by the invading countries. However, we see in Israelite history that the Jews would reclaim their homeland, rebuilding and restoring what their enemies had torn down. And so, through the example of the tent which Moses erected, the temple which Solomon built, and the restoration of that temple by different Israelite kings over the years, we must see the central point of the tent and the temple as being a *physical representation* of God's abiding presence in Israel. We must also see that any physical structure which God commanded the Israelites to build in order to "house" Him was *just a symbol*, as we know that God cannot be confined to a man-made structure. Whether it was the actual building, the creative and colorful décor that adorned the outside and inside, the physical garments upon each of the Levitical priests, or ceremonial washings and sacrifices that had to be performed upon the alters, everything God commanded the Israelites to build and perform were *types and shadows* of the coming Messiah and His spiritual Body which would be revealed through the manifestation of the Church.

The Meeting Place of the Early Church

After the advent of Christ, His life, death, resurrection, and ascension, the Jews continued the practice of meeting in the temple of their day. It was the center for prayer, worship, sacrifice, and fellowship with God. Of course, after Pentecost, the apostles of Christ began to see that the Spirit of God was not limited to a physical building anymore, as Jews all throughout Jerusalem were being filled with God's presence, empowered by His anointing, and sent around the city preaching the Gospel. And yet, we still see Peter and John on their way to the temple during the "hour of prayer" in Acts 3:1. We find in Acts 2:46 that the local church of Jerusalem "continued daily with one accord in the *temple*." Acts 5:42 declares "And daily in the *temple*, and in every house, they ceased not to teach and preach Jesus Christ." They still met in the temple because they were still upholding the Jewish tradition. The scripture does not say that they rented some store front or place of business; they had access to the temple because *they were Jews*. When Greeks wanted to go into the Jewish temple, the non-believing Jews did not receive them with open arms, but rather raised hell over the situation. In fact, after the apostle Paul brought Trophimus – a Greek disciple from Ephesus – into the temple in Jerusalem, the Jews became outraged at this and shouted, "...this is the man (Paul), that teacheth all men everywhere against the people, and the law, and this place: and further brought Greeks also into the temple, and *hath polluted this holy place.*" Notice how they saw this Greek man's presence as having "polluted" the temple. Although these Jews were unbelievers, it still reveals the mindset that those living in Jerusalem had concerning non-Jews either entering the temple, or interacting with Jews in general. This Pharisaical mindset was also still a part of many early Jewish believers. Peter had to be rebuked by Paul for "playing the hypocrite" in Galatians 2:12. Paul speaks of Peter's hypocrisy by saying, *"For before that certain came from James, he did eat with the Gentiles: but when they were come, he withdrew and separated himself, fearing them which were of the circumcision."* Peter feared being associated with the Gentiles because of the Christian Jews who were present.

In Acts 2 we find Peter at the helm of the Pentecostal outpouring in Jerusalem, and yet it is not until eight chapters later that we see Peter's mindset begin to change in regard to Christ's gift for *all* men, which included the Gentiles. In Acts 10, we find Peter on the roof of his house when he receives a vision from the Lord. A sheet with "all manner of four-footed beasts of the earth, and wild beasts, and creeping things, and fowls of the air" came descending out of heaven. He hears a voice which says "Rise, Peter; kill, and eat." To this, Peter indignantly replies "Not so, Lord; for I have never eaten anything that is common or unclean." Then, the Lord rebukes him by saying "What God hath cleansed, that call not thou common." Verse 16 reveals that this interaction between the Lord and Peter was repeated three times! Peter stubbornly refused to participate in an activity which he perceived as unclean, even though the Lord was telling him that He had cleansed it. We find out later that the animal laden sheet was just a symbol of the Gentile people. And it would be by divine design that a Gentile named Cornelius would invite Peter to his home in order that the apostle might preach the Gospel. It is of profound significance that the Spirit of God filled all those in the home as Peter spoke with them. Two things are worth mentioning here. The first is that the Holy Spirit – previously seen by the Jews as being exclusively for them – filled these Gentile people. The second is that this spiritual filling occurred *outside the temple*. This demonstrated the truth that God had in fact cleansed the Gentiles along with the Jews, and that a Gentile home was just as conducive for the Holy Spirit's presence as the Jewish temple or a Jewish home.

In addition to meeting in the temple, we know that the Jews began meeting from "house to house" as stated in Acts 2:42. There was a real *personalization* of the Gospel message and its demonstration as people began seeing God not just in their religious obligations to the temple, but even in the place where they lived. And even though the Jews still met in the temple, we must understand this point clearly – the temple was the central location for *Jewish Christians* to meet, and is not spoken of in conjunction with Gentile believers *anywhere* in the New Testament account. We find no mention of Peter encouraging Cornelius and his family to begin meeting in the temple. Furthermore, we find no mention by Paul requiring any of his Gentiles converts to meet in a temple. Nor do we find any instances where Gentiles were even encouraged to rent or buy a building to be the central location for their corporate worship.

The Immaturity of the Early Apostles' mindset

In Matthew 17, the Lord Jesus took with him Peter, James, and John to the top of a mountain where He was to be transfigured by the glory of God. As the blinding white light of heaven encompassed Him, and the prophets Elijah and Moses spoke with Him, Peter said to the Lord, *"Then answered Peter, and said unto Jesus, Lord, it is good for us to be here: if thou wilt, let us make here three tabernacles; one for thee, and one for Moses, and one for Elias"* (4). Peter wanted to build three tabernacles, one for Jesus, one for Moses, and one for Elijah. And why did he want to do this? Jesus was standing in front of them, full of the radiating glory of His Father. Two of the greatest Old Covenant prophets appeared with Him and talked with Him. The atmosphere around the mountain turned white with a heavenly shine. And all Peter could think of was building something *physical* to *house* what he was experiencing. By this, we see the carnal natured, Adamic minded, pre-Cross man at work, always attempting to build something physical to bridge the gap between divinity and humanity. We see the same human effort on the part of Nimrod, who was set on building a physical edifice high enough in order to reach heaven (see Genesis 11). What Peter did not realize at the time was that Jesus actually embodied the life of divinity in the body of humanity, bridging that impossible gap between God and man. Furthermore, Peter did not yet understand that Jesus was not looking to build a physical building in order for man to meet with God, as the Israelites had in Moses' tent and Solomon's temple.

This event on the mountain top was prior to Jesus' crucifixion, His resurrection, and His ascension into heaven. And therefore it is likely that those living in Israel at the time of Jesus' earthly life had many unanswered questions concerning the Messiah, many doubts, many misunderstandings about God's purpose for humanity. Peter and the rest of the disciples were not special in this sense, as they all exhibited fears, doubts, misunderstandings, and unbelief about many things relating to Christ's ultimate purpose of reconciling man back to God, and birthing forth the Church. Once Pentecost came, the Holy Spirit was poured out and the local church of Jerusalem was born. There had indeed been certain transformations in the disciples' hearts and minds about a great many things by that time. However, they were just beginning to see the height, depth, and breadth of God's unfolding wisdom. And just like a newborn child is a complete human being at his or her stage of life and must mature in mind and body, the Church would need to grow and mature in the wisdom and spiritual knowledge of the Christ and the Father's plan. Although Peter had experienced a great revelation of Christ's finished work on the Cross, he was still immature in his commitment to the scandalous truth that God had included Gentiles into the same righteous standing as the Jews, as seen with the example in Galatians 2:12. In the same way, there were many believers who had come out of Judaism whose minds still had the threads of the Mosaic Law hanging on. These Jewish Christians were fully included into the New Covenant, and were fully sons of God; yet, they still desired to impose circumcision upon the Gentile believers, and still had the temptation of separating from those Gentile Christians.

It wasn't until the apostle Paul was given his revelation of the Body of Christ, the mystery of union with God, and the perfection which every believer has in Christ, that a clear understanding of the absolute unity between Jew and Gentile was understood. Although the twelve apostles in Christ's earthly ministry would come to see the greatness of the Messiah, it would be through Paul – the one who was "born out of due time" – that the Church would capture the fullness of Christ's finished work.

Symbols vs. Substance

In our modern day institutional Christianity, we have been confused about the purpose of the Church meeting in part because we have carried over ideas which were prevalent in the Jewish mindset under the Old Covenant. For example, instead of seeing Christ's Body as the temple in which He dwells, we have made the *physical building* the place in which He lives. The outside of our buildings are adorned with signs and symbols in order to create the idea that "We are a church!" And yet, this only fosters a mindset throughout the community that the local church is in fact a building, an organization, some man-made institution that consists of brick and mortar. Instead of seeing segments of the tabernacle – with its outer court, inner court, and most holy place – as symbolizing various aspects of Christ's atonement for sin, priestly ministry, and glorious presence – we have patterned the inside of our buildings off of that tabernacle, creating the "outer court" in the foyer, the "inner court" in the area where the general assembly sits, and the most holy place on the stage where only those "approved" are allowed. We have also adopted Greco-Roman style format in creating row-style seating where people sit, facing those who are actively participating in music ministry, teaching, or other forms of Body ministry. This passive existence in the Church meeting creates the idea that there is a "priest-class" in Christ's Body, similar to the way the Levites were the priest-tribe of Israel, and performed the spiritual services in the presence of the Israelites. Furthermore, we make the people come to the front of the room – where the "priest-class" operates – in order to receive prayer. This further propagates the idea that only a select few are called to administer spiritual things. The fact that we have a place by the stage-area called the "alter," and that we use language like "come to the altar and receive the Lord," creates the idea that there is a legitimate alter that people must kneel to or even climb upon in order to receive atonement for their sins. We separate our children from certain parts of the service that we deem "too mature" for their ears and eyes to experience. As a result, the younger generation – teens to twenties – have been disconnected from essential revelation about Christ, and essential experience with Christ's presence. In addition to these things, the leader of the sectarian gathering will often wear a suit to distinguish him from the rest. Like the Jewish priests who wore priestly garb, this distinguishing of oneself from others is in order to create the idea that he or she is in fact someone of note, someone to be distinguished from the others, and someone who

> *We have made much ado over the symbols which pointed toward Christianity, that it has actually become difficult to see the substance of our Christianity*

carries more authority. Now, not every sectarian gathering consists of all these points, however it is true that the majority of our Church gatherings contain most if not all of these things.

The truth is that we have made much ado over the *symbols* which pointed toward Christianity, that it has actually become difficult to see the *substance* of our Christianity. If we saw the truth about the physical temple, that it was a mere *symbol* of God's habitation in man, we would eliminate the need to create a temple for the Church today. If we saw the priests who worked in the temple as *symbols* of God's spiritual priesthood, we would begin seeing every believer as already part of Christ's "royal priesthood" mentioned in 1 Peter 2:9. We would then cease from exalting a "priest-class" amongst the Church, who perform most of the spiritual service in our meetings. If we saw the colors inside the temple as a *symbol* of God's many attributes, we would not spend so much time trying to see Christ through the aesthetic designs in our buildings, but would rather begin seeing those attributes in one another. If we saw the altar of burnt offerings as a *symbol* of God's atonement for our sins, and if we saw the Cross of Christ as the altar upon which God actually removed our sins, we would not designate a part as some altar for people to come to. It is true that our close adherence to symbolism in our modern day institutions has made us dull to the divine substance which God has placed within each person. And this is why we must not seek to rebuild the types and shadows of the Old Covenant in a New Covenant age, but should rather begin living in the light of Christ's finished work on the Cross, and the Body which He has manifested in the world.

All of this *would* be mere baseless criticism if it were not for the fact that we have been conditioned to see the local church meeting as *needing all of these things.* If a sect decided to disband their organization, close the doors of their building, and meet in a home, would the people know how to operate as members of Christ's Body? If the leaders of the group did not announce their titles in front of the rest of the people, could each member still know how to see each other not "after the flesh" but "after the Spirit"? If there weren't row-seating, but rather a circle of people around a living room, could each member still feel as though he or she was in a legitimate church meeting? If we actually allowed our children to be a part of our fellowship, from start to finish, could we accommodate their immaturity? If these traditional aspects of our gatherings are not in fact needed for a group to be considered a "local church," as many will assert, why do those people feel the need to duplicate these forms and functions in order to feel as though they were a part of a legitimate church service? It is the tendency of the unrenewed mind to rebuild the forms and functions of the Old Covenant. And it is this tendency that must be changed by the revelation of the finished work of Christ.

We Are the Building

Before we see the simplicity, spontaneity, and supernatural nature of assembling together with the local church in our city, we must become convinced that the New Covenant speaks of *us* as the building of Christ. If we are in fact the building of God, then we should see a need to eliminate all of the symbolism in our meetings that detract from seeing the *substance* and *fulfillment* of those types and shadows. If we are the building of God, then there is no need to build an altar, distinguish one member from another through physical attire, or adorn our meeting rooms with the symbolism of Christianity. If we are the building of God, we ought to remove everything that keeps us from being fully persuaded that Christ has eliminated carnal divisions amongst His people, the system of external guides and laws, and has taken us out from being led by one man to being led by His Spirit.

In John 2:19, Jesus is speaking to Jews about the temple that existed in their day. He says, "Destroy this temple and in three days I will raise it up." He was revealing a provocative truth, more sublime than the Jewish mindset could even fathom. Jesus was prophesying of the destruction of His physical body, and as a result, the resurrection from the grave which He would experience three days later. Of course, the Jews did not understand His veiled language, as their unregenerate minds were trying to grasp what Christ said about raising up a building in three days, which took forty-six years to build. Jesus was saying that His very own death would be the *baptizing of the physical building* pointing to the resurrection of the spiritual building – the Body of Christ. Hebrews 3:2-6 speaks of this truth: "Who was faithful to him that appointed him, as also Moses was faithful in all his house. For this man was counted worthy of more glory than Moses, inasmuch as he who hath builded the house hath more honour than the house. For every house is builded by some man; but he that built all things is God. *And Moses verily was faithful in all his house*, as a servant, for a testimony of those things which were to be spoken after; But Christ as a son over his own house; *whose house are we*, if we hold fast the confidence and the rejoicing of the hope firm unto the end" (emphasis mine). Notice that Moses is described as being faithful in God's house whereas the Church is described *as the house of God!* This is of profound significance as it reveals the transformation that occurred with the resurrection of Christ. We have become the very substance of the Old Covenant building, housing the very

> *Jesus' intent was not to build more temples like the Jews had, but to raise up an incorruptible building that would house His Holy Spirit*

Person of God. Clearly, Jesus' intent was not to build more temples like the Jews had, but to raise up an incorruptible building that would house His Holy Spirit. The tabernacle of Moses and the temple of Solomon were merely types and shadows of this spiritually perfect, incorruptible people who would become living, breathing containers of God's glory.

The focus of the early Church meeting was not on the physical building, but on individual believers. As they got together in one place, they were seeing the spiritual reality represented in the physical temple of the Old Covenant. God dwells within His people as a fulfillment of Jesus' prayer in John 17:21 where He said, "That they all may be one; as thou, Father, art in me, and I in thee, that they also may be one in us." The point of this is to show that when we assemble together, we are not to idolize, overemphasize, or make our priority the maintaining of a physical structure, as though *that* were God's dwelling place. We are not to call the physical structure "the house of God." We are to place value upon each individual member of the Body as the temples of God. And when we come together, we are to see ourselves as the corporate expression of God's house – His Spirit living and breathing in each of us. This is essential to make clear before we speak of the kind of meeting that Christ has ordained for His Church.

Chapter Nine

The Church Meeting Part II

Within the spiritual organism called "the local church," there are various roles that each member has which reveal different facets of Christ's nature. And in order to facilitate each of those roles – whether it is prophecy, teaching, music, or hospitality – we need a specific type of gathering. Paul tells us in 1 Corinthians 12 that every member should have the ability to function within a single meeting. And by "function" we mean to express some facet of that divine nature. This gives us a clue into the nature of the biblical, local church meeting, namely that they are to be organized around the individual members and *not* around one man, or one particular ministry. If every person has a role, and every person is to be encouraged to flow in his or her gifting, then the gathering must be conducive for that kind of natural and spiritual interaction. When the meeting is centered on the "pastor," we are centering the many-membered Body of Christ on *one particular ministry*. In actuality, the pastor is not the focal point; each individual member becomes essential if the operation as a whole is to be healthy. When we observe the way in which our institutional church meetings have operated, we see that we have focused all of our attention on the stage, on the pulpit, or on those things happening in front of us. And yet, when we come together, it is essential that everyone come expecting to do something that will affect the whole group.

The context by which we gain our greatest understanding of what the local church meeting consists of is found in 1 Corinthians 12 and 14. Both of these chapters describe a detailed, multi-membered arrangement which reveals characteristics of a biblical meeting. We will spend most of our time looking at chapter 12 as it sets the tone – spiritually and physically – for what is to take place when we meet. The first point that becomes apparent is its emphasis on *spontaneity* in our gatherings. The second point is that *God has set each member* in our gatherings. The third point is that there is *more than one member* in our gatherings. And the fourth point is that there is a *plurality of ministry* in our gatherings. We will look at each of these individually.

Spontaneity

Spontaneity occurs when the Holy Spirit initiates the goings on within a local church meeting. Although every member present is ready to hear from the Lord, speak forth His word, interact with the other people, and experience demonstrations of God's presence, there is an underlying understanding that unless the Spirit speaks, reveals something to our minds, or demonstrates Himself, there can be no authentic ministry. And although many will attest to the idea that the Spirit *does* lead their services, the truth is that He can in a limited way. What the modern day church has done is to relegate the Holy Spirit's operation to a specific timeline, to a preplanned format, and to a handful of people on Sunday morning. Many people are afraid to actually allow the Spirit to lead a meeting. And so, they have effectively usurped the genuine spontaneity that comes when the Holy Spirit is initiating contact with His people and through His people. They will say "There must be order!" What they really mean to say is, "We must have *someone* calling the shots!" The fear is that if the meeting does not have some line-itemed, programmatic format, it will be chaotic or impotent. This could not be further from the truth. *Spontaneity is the sign that your gathering is being led by the Holy Spirit.* Another way to understand the idea of "spontaneity" is by expecting everything that is accomplished in a particular meeting to occur *as the Spirit wills.* Notice the pattern in each of these verses below, all taken from 1 Corinthians 12:

Vs. 3 – no man can say that Jesus is the Lord, *but by the Holy Ghost*

Vs. 4 – Now there are diversities of gifts, *but the same Spirit*

Vs. 5 – And there are differences of administrations, *but the same Lord*

Vs. 6 – And there are diversities of operations, *but it is the same God which worketh all in all*

Vs. 7 – But *the manifestation of the Spirit is given* to every man to profit withal

Vs. 8 – For to one is given by the Spirit the word of wisdom; to another the word of knowledge
by the same Spirit

Vs. 9 – To another faith *by the same Spirit;* to another the gifts of healing *by the same Spirit*

Vs. 10-11 – To another the working of miracles; to another prophecy; to another discerning of spirits; to another divers kinds of tongues; to another the interpretation of tongues: *But all these worketh that one and the selfsame Spirit, dividing to every man severally as he will*

It is the Holy Spirit's work that causes a person to say "Jesus is Lord." It is the Holy Spirit's work that weaves together every gift in the room. It is the Holy Spirit's work to distinguish various administrations in the group. It is the Holy Spirit's work to exercise different operations within a meeting. It is the Holy Spirit's work to manifest Himself through each person. It is the Holy Spirit's work to release the word of wisdom and the word of knowledge through individual people. It is the Holy Spirit's work to initiate faith in each member's heart, and to administer healing to the sick. It is the Holy Spirit's work to divide up His abilities in each member. All of these things work because it is the Holy Spirit's responsibility to initiate the divine nature in and through Christ's Body. Since He is the great initiator of ministry in the Church, we must see that *spontaneity* is the chief characteristic in our meetings. Because we cannot muster up faith on our own, healings on our own, operations of the power on our own, or prophecy on our own, we become totally dependent upon the Holy Spirit's spontaneous work when we come together.

> *We must come to see spontaneity as the chief characteristic in our meetings*

Another way to understand the crucial nature of the Holy Spirit's spontaneous nature in our meetings is to consider a physical body. Upon a basic study, we know that the head contains the brain which acts as the "control center," releasing signals to individual muscles which cause our bodies to move. This is significant as the body cannot move without receiving signals from the brain. Christ is the Head of the spiritual Body called "the Church." As such, any movement in His Body must originate in the mind of Christ. Since Christ is the Head of His Body and the mind of His Church, we understand that our individual movements in a meeting are determined by the supernatural signals that He gives to us, spontaneously and in the moment.

In 1 Corinthians 12:11 we read, "But all these worketh that one and the selfsame Spirit, dividing to every man severally as he will." Notice the emphasis here is on the Spirit's will, *not* the individual's will. The will of the Spirit determines who will be functioning in what gift, in any particular meeting. A leader such as the apostle Paul can recognize *how* the Spirit moves in different members, and upon recognizing that movement, distinguish those individuals according to what he perceives about them; however a leader's perception and recognition of each individual is *not required* for those members to function. We know that Paul spoke of the different ministries that are possible in a given meeting. He said that there may be prophesies, revelation, music, teaching, and so on. It is likely that someone like Paul was able to perceive who was gifted as a teacher, who was apt to share a revelation, and who might be able to provide musical worship. However, Paul's recognition of these gifts, and his outlining them in 1 Corinthians 12, 14, along with Romans 12 and Ephesians 4, *does not* mean that he was the one who allowed or prohibited these ministries from functioning. He was simply making the Church aware of what God had done to create "diversities of gifts," "difference of administrations," and "diversities of operations."

Those whom we consider "leaders" must not police the local church, but rather should be facilitators of each member's gift. And by "facilitating" we mean that they are to recognize who is laboring amongst them and *allow them room to minister*. It is not the job of the facilitator to start and stop ministry, but to recognize ministry as it is revealed by the Holy Spirit. It is the job of the Holy Spirit to start and stop ministry, however He will use the facilitator to encourage those in the meeting to minister. In a sense, these meetings are led *passively* in that we as people are always dependent upon the help of the Holy Spirit. Although we may set a specific time aside for people to gather, recognize those who are among us, and be confident in what God has called us to do, we are still to let the Holy Spirit lead the meeting as He is our leader in all things. The result of His leadership is that there will be many spontaneous things arising in our meetings.

We must give up control and allow people to minister – even to make mistakes. This will provide a great platform for correction, while not dampening people's fire to actually minister. The apostle Paul did provide instructions on what a church meeting should contain, and even included correction on some of the *wrong ways* in which the local churches gathered (see 1 Corinthians 11). Even though the Corinthians, for example, had incidents of immaturity and carnality in their midst, he continually affirmed them nonetheless, and encouraged them to continue using their various gifts, operations, and administrations without imposing man-made hurdles on their charismatic progress. At the end of the day, the Church belongs to Jesus Christ, and whereas leadership may confront immaturity, they should not ultimately hinder the spontaneity of the Holy Spirit who will flow through mature and immature vessels alike.

God Sets the Members

According to 1 Corinthians 12:18, God has set each member in His Body. We read, "But now hath God set the members every one of them in the body, as it hath pleased him." Individuals are placed within Christ's Body according to God's design, God's wisdom, and God's pleasure. We did not become a part of the Church because we decided to stop getting drunk, stealing money, or because we showed up to a service one Sunday morning. We were snatched from a life of sin and from the grip of Satan because Christ took away our sin and destroyed the works of the devil (see 1 John 3:5 & 8). There was a point in time that we awoke to the righteousness of Christ's accomplishment, and we saw our old life of sin as having been removed at the Cross. In the same way that our salvation from sin and the devil came as a grace gift, so also is our membership in Christ's Body a grace gift. The moment we became aware of Christ's life, death, and resurrection, and believed upon His finished work, it was as if we awoke from a lifelong slumber and were introduced to reality for the first time. We awoke to find ourselves grafted into the Christ-vine, placed into a heavenly society, and made a member of a spiritual Body. Since our origination into Christ came by the grace of God, we must see that everything else in our spiritual lives has to be initiated by the same grace. Our functioning as a teacher, a prophet, or an exhorter, was awakened in us by God – not by man, or by some human agency. We cannot "make" someone a teacher, a prophet, or an exhorter. Likewise, we

> *All of these graces originate in Christ and must be seen as initiated by God in every local church*

cannot "make" someone evangelize, teach, or exhort. The gifts of God are gifts *from* God, and therefore are released *by* God. In the same way that each member of Christ's Body originated *in Christ*, the ministry that each member possesses originates *in Christ*. God has placed within each local church, teachers, administrators, and evangelists. He has given each local church those with a special grace for mercy, giving, and exhortation. He has anointing individuals for music, hospitality, and the working of miracles. All of these graces originate in Christ and must be seen as initiated by God in every local church.

All that is left for us to do is to *recognize* those whom God has set in our midst. This is precisely why Paul commands us to "know them which labor among you." This "knowing" is not a mere knowledge that there is another person in the room with you; it is a *discerning of who this person is in Christ*, and *what purpose they serve in the church meeting*. This takes spiritual eyes to see, even as Paul commands us to know "no man after the flesh" (see 2 Corinthians 5:16). In other words, we are to have an intimate knowledge of our "left hand" and our "right hand," – those we are in fellowship with – so that we can experience unity in Christ's Body as well as appreciation for the spiritual diversities within our local church. Upon knowing those members that function by our side, we are actively discerning the Body of Christ, as we are commanded to do in 1 Corinthians 11. Since each person has a supply of the Spirit, and has been placed by God into our gatherings, we cannot help but allow them to operate in the way Christ has intended. Upon operating in that way, everyone in the gathering will become edified by the prophecy, teaching, exhortation, and whatever else the Spirit desires to do.

Paul understood that the Church belonged to Christ. He understood that there were many members in Christ's Body. And so, he knew that even if a group of believers were immature in their revelation of how perfect they were, and occasionally forgot that they had been liberated from their sinful flesh, they *still* belonged to Christ. Ultimately, Paul constructed his letters to, on the one hand, deal with the immaturity that certain local churches were manifesting, and on the other hand, make sure that they understood their membership was not conditional on their works – righteous or unrighteous – but was based solely on Christ's desire to include them into His Body. And so, Paul still encouraged the churches to function as members of that Body, while at the same time relating the need for them to remain holy and throw off fleshly works.

More Than One Member

In the apostolic journeys of Paul, Peter, John, and the other apostles, we find their missions taking them to unchurched nations, cities, and people. Although it is hard to fit their experiences into our churched culture in America, we must still see the underlying idea behind their preaching – to see individuals liberated from their own darkened state and awakened to the reality of Christ's kingdom. If only two people within a city believe the good news that we are preaching, they will still constitute the beginning of the local church in that city. This does not mean that this particular local church has to remain with only two members, but it signifies the importance of seeing those two individuals as part of the Body. Now, as part of Christ's Body, those two members may go forth and preach to others within that city and see more added to that local church. As the church grows, so grows its membership. The point is that there is more than one member that makes up the local church. In 1 Corinthians 12:12, Paul says, "For as the body is one, *and hath many members*, and all the members of that one body, being many, *are one body*: so also is Christ" (emphasis mine). This reveals that there is more than one member who should be functioning in the local church meeting, *and* that there is complete unity amongst each member. Paul further emphasizes this point in verse 20 by saying, "But now are they many members, yet but one body." Understanding that there is more than one member in the local church may seem elementary, but the reason Paul mentions it and makes a point of emphasizing it, is to show that no one member is exalted over another, no one member is more needed than another, and no one member is more important in the corporate growth of the Body. It is a sad fact that many in the Church are still immature on this point. Whereas it is right to distinguish members as having unique and differing roles in their respective callings, it is an unnoticed sin when we gravitate toward one more than another, when we exalt more visibly charismatic members, and when we separate "clergy" from "laity" creating a caste system in the local church. "More than one member" signifies not only more than one person functioning in the local churches, but implies that each member is equally as valuable, equally as needed, equally as part of Christ's plan for the Church.

Plurality of Ministry

1 Corinthians 14:26 says, "How is it then, brethren? when ye come together, every one of you hath a psalm, hath a doctrine, hath a tongue, hath a revelation, hath an interpretation. Let all things be done unto edifying." Notice here that Paul is highlighting *three different but related characteristics of the local church meeting*. The first is that we are to "come together." There is no way around individuals actually meeting in some geographic location within a city, to be the corporate expression of Christ's Body. The second is that "every one of you" has a functioning role in the local church meeting. Whether it is a

psalm, a doctrine, a tongue, a revelation, or an interpretation, everyone should be ready to minister as the Holy Spirit leads them. Much like a symphonic orchestra where there are many instruments overlapping their harmonies, arranged to complement each other and bring diversity to a song while not detracting from the individual notes and instruments, there is absolute unity in the diversity of members within a local church meeting. One person may have a particular leaning toward prophecy, whereas another toward musical song; however their differing leanings does not mean that they are at odds with one another, but rather that they are meant to complement one another. And third, each individual ministry should be "done unto edifying." God has given each person a ministry to build the local church; we have not been called to build up a person's ministry, rather to use the ministry we've received to build the local church. When we put all these together, we find a real *plurality of ministry* in the local church meeting. By "plurality," we mean that there is more than one person ministering, more than one person with a word, and more than one person with a significant voice. The apostle Paul declares in 1 Corinthians 14:31 that, "For ye may all prophesy one by one, that all may learn, and all may be comforted." Notice here that "all" may prophesy. By "all," Paul is speaking of every person that is present in the church meeting. This does not mean that everyone *must* have a prophecy, but implies that everyone *can* have something to minister.

Now, there are clearly differing roles within the local church. Not everyone is a teacher in the local church, and therefore not everyone should assume the role of teaching doctrine to people. Not everyone is a prophet in the local church, and therefore not everyone should call themselves "prophet" simply because they can *prophesy*. Although there are differing roles within the local church, and not everyone is called as a teacher, prophet, or pastor, these differences do not diminish the main point of 1 Corinthians 12 and 14 which is that *all* may minister something from the Holy Spirit, and should not be prevented simply because they are *not* a teacher, prophet, or pastor. The mindset of whoever is facilitating meetings must be to accommodate *all members* of Christ's Body. There must be a strong emphasis on *every part* so that the group as a whole can be refreshed, nourished, and built up in their identity. Only when every member is allowed to function can there be the kind of growth – in terms of maturity and in terms of physical numbers – that the Church so desires.

Decently and In Order

One of the most commonly held up scriptures used in relation to the church meeting is found in 1 Corinthians 14:40. We read, "Let all things be done decently and in order." This instruction comes at the end of two very detailed chapters on the way in which the local church is to meet (1 Corinthians 12 & 14). Where the Church at large has gone wrong is to interpret the idea of "order" as meaning the kind of order we find in worldly institutions. We have been taught that "order" means that we need to construct some man-made, hierarchical organization that props up one man at the top who leads like a CEO, and sets up institutional walls around the local church. We take "order" to mean that our meetings should be air-tight, allowing no room for anything spontaneous, anything unplanned, or anyone who is not scheduled to minister. We have believed that "order" is the elimination of any "spilled milk" in our services, as we have become professional "church meeting organizers," scheduling everything that will happen ahead of time. However, this is *not* what the apostle Paul meant when he said "let everything be done decently and in order." By "order," Paul was not trying to get the local church to follow some religious liturgy where the music ministry comes first, and then the teaching, and then the praying – we find no such "order of service" laid out in his instruction. By "order," he was not speaking of some human government taking control of the local church meeting, setting

> *We are to let everything be done decently and in order so that each member has an opportunity to minister*

up individuals as CEO's of the local church affairs. In the context of 1 Corinthians 12:3-11, 1 Corinthians 12:18, 1 Corinthians 12:12, and 1 Corinthians 14:26, the "order" Paul speaks about is referring to the *spontaneity of the Spirit*, the fact that *God sets every member*, that *there are many members*, and that *there is plurality of ministry* all within the local church meeting. In other words, we are to let everything be done decently and in order so that *each member has an opportunity to minister*! And, we are to let everything be done decently and in order so that those who are ministering are not hindered or interrupted but are allowed to flow according to the Spirit's will. Of course, we have thought that the pastor must never be interrupted, and that *his* ministry takes precedent. This is not the case! The pastor may have a teaching for the group, however he must be equally attentive to the other members of the gathering so that *he does not interrupt or hinder their ministry*! Furthermore, we must see that "order" in our meetings does not always look like everyone sitting neatly in their seat, everyone's eyes fixed on one person, or everyone keeping silent. If the Holy Spirit wants everyone on the floor, a line of people speaking prophetic utterance, or a song to break into the middle of the meeting, then *that* is order. If the Holy Spirit wants the main teacher to yield the time to another who has a revelation from the Lord, then *that* is order. If the Holy Spirit wants silence for 30 minutes, then *that* is order. This does not mean that *nothing* should be planned, but that we are truly allowing for every member to minister, for the spontaneity of the Spirit to direct the meeting, and for every person to be mutually edified and exercised.

Lastly, when we survey chapters 12 and 14 of 1 Corinthians, we find that Paul spends most of his time talking about the *content* of a local church meeting, and devotes virtually no time to how it is to be arranged. Paul understood that if the Holy Spirit was truly leading a group of believers, then all of the things he outlined would occur. Of course, at the very end of the outlining we find Paul saying "let all things be done decently and in order." This instruction was necessary for both the immature believer who will tend to interrupt a meeting, as well as the ignorant pastor who will tend to dominate and disallow the other believers to flow as the Spirit wills. Paul purposely left out the *arrangement* of the local church meeting, because when we focus on trying to arrange all of the content in our gatherings – whether they be gifts, operations or administrations – we head down the road to dry, uninspired, and formulaic gatherings. We must remember that these meetings are led by the Holy Spirit, and therefore we baptize ourselves afresh in creativity, power, and demonstration of unity by always acknowledging our submission to His leadership, particularly in His ability to arrange what will take place and in what order.

References

CHAPTER ONE

1 Blue Letter Bible. "Dictionary and Word Search for paradosis (Strong's G3862)". Blue Letter Bible. 1996-2014. 24 Oct 2014. <http://www.blueletterbible.org/lang/lexicon/lexicon.cfm?Strongs=G3862&t=KJV>

CHAPTER TWO

1 "Nation." Merriam Webster. n.p., n.d. Web 27 Oct 2014.

CHAPTER THREE

1 Blue Letter Bible. "Dictionary and Word Search for teleo (Strong's G5055)". Blue Letter Bible. 1996-2014. 27 Oct 2014. <http://www.blueletterbible.org/lang/lexicon/lexicon.cfm?Strongs=G5055&t=KJV>

CHAPTER SIX

1 "Sect." Merriam Webster. n.p., n.d. Web. 27 Oct 2014.

2 Blue Letter Bible. "Dictionary and Word Search for hairesis (Strong's G139)". Blue Letter Bible. 1996-2014. 27 Oct 2014. < http://www.blueletterbible.org/lang/lexicon/lexicon.cfm?Strongs=G139&t=KJV>

www.ingramcontent.com/pod-product-compliance
Lightning Source LLC
Chambersburg PA
CBHW060804050426
42449CB00008B/1521